# Tripping on the Color Line

# Tripping on the Color Line

## Black-White Multiracial Families in a Racially Divided World

*Heather M. Dalmage*

**Rutgers University Press**

New Brunswick, New Jersey, and London

Library of Congress Cataloging-in-Publication Data

Dalmage, Heather M., 1965–
    Tripping on the color line : Black-white multiracial families in a
racially divided world / c Heather M. Dalmage.
    p.  cm.
    Includes bibliographical references and index.
    ISBN 0-8135-2843-7 (alk. paper)
    1. Interracial marriage—United States.  2. Racially mixed
children—United States.  3. United States—Social conditions.
4. United States—Race relations.  I. Title.

HQ1031.D34 2000
306.84'6—dc21

                                                00-032350

British Cataloging-in-Publication data for this book is available from
the British Library

Second paperback printing, 2003

Manufactured in the United States of America

*To my parents,*
*Dorothea L. Trepanier*
*and*
*Lionel G. Trepanier*

# Contents

# Acknowledgments

This book would not have been possible without the efforts and patience of many. Because of the open and honest participation of multiracial family members—their words, ideas, and various understandings of the world—I have been able to think about race differently. Many people welcomed me graciously into their homes. Others traveled distances to meet with me and share their stories. And since the interviews were conducted in two parts, my double thanks to everyone. Irene Rottenberg, a founder of GIFT in Montclair, New Jersey, opened up her home and welcomed me for meetings and discussions. Irene Carr, a founder of the BFN, took the time to share the history of the organization and also welcomed me for meetings and discussions.

Thanks to my parents, Lionel and Dorothea Trepanier, who have always been supportive and encouraging. My brothers and sisters—Lionel Trepanier, Ray Trepanier, Jessie Mougette, and Owen Trepanier—have all extended needed support. In particular, I thank my older sister, Anna Stange. Her insights, suggestions, and editing mark nearly every page of this book. In addition, she has given me peace of mind by taking wonderful care of my daughter, Mahalia, so that I could have extra time to write.

Many thanks to friends and colleagues who have helped me along the way. Barbara Katz Rothman, my friend and mentor, gives me constant encouragement, challenges me to think differently about issues, and is always willing to listen. Robin Isserles read and thoroughly commented on this book in various stages, despite her busy schedule. Wendy Simonds has remained supportive and helpful throughout the project. My reading group at CUNY helped me get this book off the ground; my thanks to go out to Renate Reimann, Margarita Zambrosa, and Pamela Donovan. I would like to extend a special and overdue thank you to Felix Padilla, who taught me the ropes of qualitative research and the importance of writing accessibly. Thanks also to Bill Kornblum and Leith Mullings for their help in the initial stages of this book. Abby Ferber provided many detailed and helpful insights that helped make the book more coherent. And thanks to David Cann, Jeffrey Edwards, Denise Ingram, David Myers, Silvia Perez, Patricia Sugrue, and LaShawn West, who each provided valuable criticism. The Dissertation Fellowship Committee at the City University of New York's Graduate Center and the Summer Grant Committee at Roosevelt University both provided much-appreciated financial assistance.

Finally, I would like to thank Philip for his love, encouragement, sense of humor, and good cooking. These four qualities have helped me get through both this book and daily life and give me hope as we embark on our journey together with our baby girl, Mahalia.

# Tripping on the Color Line

# Introduction

## Thinking

## about the

## Color Line

About mid-semester during one of the introduction to sociology courses I teach, two of my cousins decided to sit in on the class. This was my first semester teaching in Chicago, and they wanted to see their "cuz" in action. At the next class meeting the students and I were sitting in a circle discussing some sociological point when the question came up: "Professor, what are you? I was talking to some people about this class, and they asked me what you are, you know, racially. I told them I wasn't sure." Another student joined in: "Yeah, what are you?"

The question is loaded. More than five hundred years' worth of socially, politically, economically, and culturally created racial categories rest in the phrase "what are you." People seeing me in the street would have little doubt that I was a white woman. Yet the cousins who sat in on my class are mixed Korean and Filipino, my aunt is Filipino, my uncle is Korean, my nieces are mixed Indonesian and white, my in-laws are Jamaican, my husband is black. What does that make me? The quick answer is "a white woman from a multiracial family." Nevertheless, the quick answer cannot address more than five hundred years of racial baggage. In a sociology course we can delve into some of this baggage and begin to address race on a more complex level. In day-to-day living, however, race is often used as a clear-cut, unambiguous way of categorizing human beings. Those of us who do not come from or live in single-race families must daily negotiate a racialized and racist system that demands we fit ourselves into prescribed categories.

When I decided to begin the research for this book, I knew few people in my shoes. My husband (a black man) and I (a white woman) had been together for nearly a decade. I had heard the question "What about the children?" so many times that I finally decided to explore the question myself. I began speaking with multiracial adults about their lives. As I listened to and talked with these individuals, I began to recognize some similarities between their experiences as multiracial people and my own as an interracially married white woman. At the same time I was participating in an adoption reading group and spending a great deal of time researching, discussing, and writing about families created through transracial adoption. It was becoming clear that multiracial people, transracially adopted people, and all members of first-generation multiracial families share many experiences in a racially unjust and segregated society. It further became evident that *family* has been a primary means through which a racially divided and racist society has been maintained.

Over the past decade, perhaps no other social institution has received as much public attention as the family. Politicians like to sweep social problems into a neat pile and dump them into the family basket. No problem is too great or small to blame on the family: overweight children, poor grades, improper nutrition, juvenile delinquency, unemployment, drug abuse, illiteracy, violence, moral decay, and the nation's inability to compete in a global economy. The underlying belief is that good families are the key to a good society. Ignored in all the political (and religious) rhetoric about the need for good families is the historical construction of family in the United States.

In traditional thinking and law, a good family is Christian, white, and middle class with a male patriarch, a chaste and virtuous housewife, and obedient children.[1] These ideologies and laws have existed side by side with laws denying African Americans (and others) the rights of marriage and family. In fact, masters often used emotional ties between slaves as a form of coercion. If a slave did not submit to a master's wishes, the master would threaten to sell, rape, or beat another slave; and children were commonly sold away from their mothers.

When slavery was abolished, African Americans gained the legal right to marry without a master's permission. Unfortunately, for many blacks emancipation meant nothing more than sharecropping. Denied jobs in factories and other arenas, they were often forced to work for a landowner who wielded a great deal of power over black families. For instance, even in prosperity, a landowner would not allow a mother to stay in the home and fulfill the role of good woman but forced her and her children to work in the fields. Outside the rural south, black men were systematically denied access to well-paying jobs and fair wages. Thus, most black women were forced to enter the labor market to survive.

All the while, industrialization was creating a framework for a white middle class in which women were defined as good so long as they stayed at home and made the family the center of their existence. Men were defined as good so long as they provided economically for their families. These white, middle-class, nuclear families were given ideological, political, economic, and social support and held up as models of virtue and perfection. In circular fashion, nuclear families were used as the justification for the privileges granted to whites and for the hostility and terror directed toward blacks (and some working-class whites). Denied economic and political resources, black families were treated like the cancer eating away at the backbone of good society.

How do any of us know what to call ourselves racially? Many people will say, "I am what my parents are and what their parents were before them and so on." In short, a popular ideology is that we know our race by our family tree. Of course, this family tree does not grow in thin air. It grows in a society that defines race in particular ways. For many years, the concept of family was legally used to maintain white supremacy by drawing a strict line between white families and all other families. In *Race and Mixed Race,* Naomi Zack argues that "the concept of race has to do with white families—more precisely, with how white family is conceptualized."[2] The traditionally enforced ideology is that a white person is pure so long as he or she has no known relatives or ancestors of color. The flip side is that having one known black ancestor makes you black.[3] The two definitions seem to account for everyone. You are white or not, black or not; there is no in between. Antimiscegenation laws (those banning marriage between whites and blacks) were set up to maintain the myth of white racial purity and superiority. While laws banning interracial marriage varied from state to state, interracial marriage has been illegal for a good part of our history. Not until 1967, buttressed by the strength of the civil rights movement, did the U.S. Supreme Court strike down antimiscegenation laws as unconstitutional.[4]

In light of the history of race and family, blacks and

whites respond very differently to contemporary discussions of multiracialism in the United States. Unlike many whites, most black Americans are aware of the history of the one-drop rule and the myth of white purity. Thus, blacks generally respond more guardedly to claims of multiracialism. For instance, when I talk about my research with black friends and colleagues, many tell me: "All African Americans are multiracial. Why do you want to create and give meaning to a separate category?" And, "I can trace my ancestry. I know which great-grandmothers were raped by white men, and I know who those white men were. But I'm still black." And, "Most African Americans are multiracial, but it is not something we like to talk about or want to celebrate. For us it is a painful history of rape, rejection, and exploitation."

Just the other day I was talking with a colleague who asked, "Do you believe there is a difference between being multiracial and being black?" I said yes.

"But," he contested, "black families and black people are multiracial, so how can you make such a distinction?"

I gave him my standard response: "Most multiracial families today are not created through rape and exploitation. Instead, we come together out of mutual respect, love, and admiration. We choose to be together, and some make great sacrifices to be together. Because of who we are in relation to each other racially, we have to fight to be a family. Larger rules of race work to divide us. Besides, our day-to-day experiences are different from the experiences of people who come from families that define themselves monoracially."

He replied, "I still think y'all just want to separate yourselves from black folks. . . . You want to say you're better than blacks."

I understood my colleague's argument. According to the traditional definition of *white family*, multiracial fam-

ilies and people are not considered white. So why are we trying to muddy the waters and claim that our experiences are
different? Shouldn't we stake a claim on the side of justice
and define ourselves as black families?

If the story ended there, life for multiracial family members would not be much different from the lives of families
who consider themselves black. But the story does continue. Black Americans have not passively received the
abuses of white supremacy. Instead, they have struggled to
unify themselves and fight the injustices of a racist society.
By unifying, they have drawn boundaries. A black professor
in a local university explained to me one day: "See, the
black community wants your husband and your children. We
don't have any use for you." In short, the one-drop rule is a
downward principle; it does not move upward or across. A
white parent or partner is not considered black by most in
the black community because he or she has no ancestral
claim to blackness. That person can walk away at any time.
Yet many whites see the white partner or parent, especially
if she is a white women, as no longer white. At the same time,
African Americans may view the entire multiracial family
with suspicion, even disdain. By disregarding the rules of race
and claiming respect for our multiracial families, we are perceived as race traitors and wishy-washy crossovers.

Antimiscegenation laws were struck down in 1967, yet
multiracial families still face a great deal of discrimination
in society. In 1984 a Florida court took child custody away
from a white mother because her second marriage was interracial. The child's biological father (a white man), who was
upset about the interracial marriage, sued for custody and
won. In the *Michigan Law Review*, Kim Forde-Mazrui notes:
"The court relied exclusively on the interracial marriage,
which, the court concluded, would subject the child to
racial hostility."[5] More recently, a white principal in Widowee,

Alabama, caught the nation's attention when he told students during an assembly that he was going to ban interracial couples from attending a school dance. When a multiracial student asked who she could go to the dance with, he replied that she was a "mistake." On New York's Long Island, a white mother with multiracial children came home to find her house spray-painted with racial slurs. In early 2000, Bob Jones University made the headlines because of its ban on interracial dating.

The percentage of interracial marriages, particularly between blacks and whites, remains low. Fewer than 1 percent of whites and 3 percent of blacks are in black-white marriages. Despite their small (albeit growing) numbers, however, black-white multiracial families receive more attention than do other multiracial families. The fact that black-white families receive disproportionate attention speaks to the seemingly immutable connection between the one-drop rule, the myth of white racial purity, and the construction of race and family in the United States.

Although many multiracial and multiethnic families come from backgrounds other than black and white, I am focusing on black-white family members for two reasons. First, blacks form the only group that has been held to the one-drop standard, and whites form the only group for which purity is believed to be the admission ticket. Second, black-white multiracial families have a unique history in the United States because of the legacy of slavery, and black-white familial relations (or the regulation of such relations) have been inextricably linked to white supremacist and patriarchal power. Thus, black-white families can serve as a lens through which to explore the implications of a growing multiracial population in a race-conscious and racist society.

In 1995 I began interviewing members of multiracial families in the Chicago and New York City areas. During the next year I interviewed forty-seven people and accumulated more than 150 hours of recorded interviews. I participated in one multiracial organization and sat on the board of directors of another. With my micro-recorder in hand, I met people in their homes, my home, their workplaces, local diners, and parks. I gained much insight because of their openness and willingness to share the details of their lives. Some of these people have become friends and collaborators. The stories I relate in this book, including my own, come from people who live in or have grown up in black-white multiracial families. We come from all walks of life. Some have been adopted into multiracial families, some are interracially married, some are parents of multiracial children, and others have parents of different races. We differ along lines of race, class, gender, sexual orientation, culture, religion, family structure, geographical location, education, and political perspective. In fact, our differences are so great that it is sad to learn how similar our experiences are. These similarities highlight the continued centrality of race in the United States and the ways in which the concept of family has been used to maintain a racially divided and racist society. Throughout this book, I incorporate the stories and ideas shared by the people I interviewed. Through the interviews I explore how race, created through human interaction, permeates every aspect of life from individual thoughts, identities, and desires to community building, social institutions, and policies. At times the interviews are used to exemplify a point. At other times they provide an insight into racial thinking and dynamics that require further analysis. Among the experiences of others, I incorporate my own experiences as a white, interracially married mother. I agree with Abby Ferber's suggestion that "attempts to ignore our own role in the social construction of race reproduce race as a natural and given category of identity."[6] My writings, my attempts to influence race debates,

come from a particular set of experiences and racial understandings of the world.

## The Color Line Defined

In *The Souls of Black Folks*, W.E.B. Du Bois predicted
that the color line would be the problem of the twentieth century. Nearly a hundred years later, at the beginning of the
twenty-first century, the color line remains a pressing social
and personal issue. While ultimately about power, identity,
and community, the color line is a difficult concept to
define. The way in which the line is drawn reflects the
racial picture being created.

Historically, several prominent conceptions of race have
been created. Racial essentialists locate race within the
human body. Social constructionists understand race as a significant and central social phenomenon that is given meaning through human thought and interaction. Color-blind
advocates draw on essentialism or social constructionism (or
both) to deny or downplay the significance of race.

### The Essentialist Color Line

Racial essentialism is the belief that humans can be
grouped together based on some shared and static quality. It
is grounded in the belief that racial groups are reflections of
genetic codes rather than social creations and hinges on
two primary ideas: first, that our racial designation is determined by DNA; second, that the DNA that codes for physical features such as skin color can indicate much more
about who a person really is. Racial essentialists cite "obvious" differences in physical features and then link physical
appearance to differences in blood pressure or predisposition
to particular diseases (such as sickle-cell anemia) as well as
differences in musical tastes, athletic ability, and speech pat-

terns.[7] Each of these differences is then used as proof that the races are essentially different.

In *Genetic Maps and Human Imaginations: The Limits of Science in Understanding Who We Are,* Barbara Katz Rothman addresses the problem of citing predisposition to particular diseases as proof that race exists in the human body. "Sickle-cell is thought of as a black or African disease, although it is not equally distributed through African populations. Within the United States, people of African descent, Italians and Greeks, are more likely to be sickle-cell carriers."[8] If we are going to cite DNA-coded disease as proof that race is a genetic phenomenon, how do we explain why Italians and Greeks are generally considered white in the United States? Where one group begins and the next ends depends on which criteria are used (or overlooked). This leads to a second shortcoming of essentialist arguments: skin color and ancestry can provide clues about what social situations a person might face in a racist society but do not tell us about an individual's culture, politics, morals, education, intelligence, athletic ability, or class.[9] For instance, we know that, based on skin color, a white male will have a much better chance of catching a cab than will a black male. In this case, skin color gives us a clue that white men do not have to spend as much time or energy getting from one location to another. We can also surmise that these cab-catching white men don't have to worry about being late for an appointment because of racism. Skin color does not, however, tell us who is rich or poor; who is a Republican, a Democrat, or a Socialist. It does not tell us who is xenophobic, sexist, or homophobic. It does not tell us who can dance well, who is uptight, who is smart, or who can jump. Skin color actually tells us very little. We can find social patterns tied to skin color and physical features, but social patterns tell us more about social structures than about individuals within the categories.[10]

Race is not inherent to individuals, yet essentialist arguments continue to play a prominent role in our society. Essentialist, "scientific" explanations have been used to justify colonization, slavery, and genocide.[11] If society is seen as a direct reflection of the inherent characteristics of different races, then white privilege is not at all about social injustice. Rather, it is a reflection of the natural order—injustice justified.[12] At the same time, however, essentialist thinking has been employed by oppressed groups as a way to create unity, strength, and solidarity in the struggle for social justice. Here the suggestion is "We all share in a similar oppression because society has cast us into one pot. We are treated with a similar disrespect and discrimination, and thus we have a shared set of experiences that inform who we are and who we should be." Unfortunately, the essentialist color line, even when used in a struggle for justice, is often based on ideas about what constitutes authentic thoughts and actions. Individuals are expected to claim racial identities that match the racial category into which they are born.[13] Those who cannot conform (or refuse to conform) are often shunned by the community or group. The color line, according to essentialists, is stark and clear.

### The Socially Constructed Color Line

Social constructionists argue that race has been created and re-created through human interaction and struggles for power and has real and consistent consequences in our lives. In *White by Law: The Legal Construction of Race*, Ian Haney Lopez notes that "meaning-systems, while originally only ideas, gain force as they are reproduced in the material conditions of society."[14] Day by day we all create race through our thoughts and actions as we assign and attach meaning to various physical features. The assigning of meaning, however, extends beyond individual thought and action. Power-laden categories created within the context of human interaction have been institutionalized. Race is central to the workings of society and, as Abby Ferber writes, it "is a social category, constructed in different times and places for different political purposes."[15] Definitions of racial categories arise from historically created social arrangements, which in turn inform and shape individual experiences. Our interactions are guided both by what we have learned about race as it intersects with other socially meaningful categories (for example, gender, class, and sexual orientation) and the real and consistent consequences that race has in our lives. Social constructionists, then, may understand the color line as fleeting and static, universal and particular, tangible and false, apparent and imagined, clear and ambiguous.[16] If the color line in question is demarcating housing, educational, and economic institutions, it is clearer, starker, and bolder. If it is demarcating individuals, it becomes blurred. An individual's relationship to the color line is seen as a process, something tied closely to lived experiences.

A socially constructed color line with recognized complexities makes the struggle for justice difficult. Some sense of unity, of an "us," is necessary when groups are struggling for greater justice. This sense of community is necessary for both countering the feelings of alienation created by oppression and building political struggles. When more than one identity or set of experiences is recognized, community boundaries begin to blur, and a sense of unity becomes difficult to achieve. Thus, communities require boundaries, and boundaries require some notion of essentialism—a shared "us." Unfortunately, essentialism creates alienation by ignoring (or degrading) some experiences while privileging others. Those who don't quite fit into the prevailing notions of community are often jettisoned to the margins. For instance, unity created around issues of racial justice often subsume or ignore other differences such as gender, sexuality, and class. The experiences of multiracial family members highlight both the problems of essentialism and the complexities of social constructionism.

### The Color-Blind Color Line

In an attempt to move away from justifying injustices or demanding conformity, many people have drawn a color-blind line, denying that race is a central organizing principle in society. They either ignore the fact that race exists or subsume race under other explanations for injustice. Many color-blind advocates believe that once the layers of socially created difference are peeled away, all humans are the same, equal.[17] The path to this goal requires denying that differences exist, as in "I don't care if you are yellow, pink, green, or purple" (as if such colors have any meaning in a racist system) or "There is only one race: the human race." Nevertheless, while there may be one race, only some members of that race can catch a cab on 42nd Street.

Some have suggested that race matters because individuals continue to use language couched in racism and racial essentialism. For instance, in *The Racialization of America*, Yehudi Webster points to the way in which the media, politicians, and academics build careers by highlighting racial differences.[18] He argues that race continues to matter in society because people think, talk, write, and theorize in racial terms. In his opinion, if we stop talking about racial differences, race will cease to matter.

Race is indeed constructed through human interaction. As Michael Omi and Howard Winant remind us, however, race is central to society and extends beyond human interaction. Moreover, the discussion of differences is not the problem. The fact that we don't share the same physical features, cultural traditions, or religious beliefs is not the problem. The problem concerns the assignment of power to these differences. People designated white receive unearned privileges while those designated of color face oppression. Ignore race and we ignore the problems of inequality and injustice.

Some people suggest that while race is an important factor, it is not central to creating and maintaining inequalities in society. This version of the color-blind perspective subsumes race under class or ethnicity.[19] A common class-based argument is that race, created in a capitalist system, has been used to drive wages down. Workers—white, black, and others of color—are pitted against each other for jobs and wages. The antagonism between the so-called races then keeps the working class divided, unable to fight collectively for better working and living conditions. Omi and Winant point out the shortcomings of this argument: "Historically speaking, the call for class unity across racial lines has amounted in practice to an argument that non-whites give up their racially based demands in favor of 'class' unity on white terms."[20]

One popular ethnicity argument suggests that, given enough time, all groups will assimilate into the mainstream (white) U.S. culture. I have heard this argument most often in conversations between whites: for example, "My grandparents came over with nothing and made it. They didn't speak the language and didn't have an education, but they worked long, hard hours in bad jobs and made it." The problem with this line of reasoning is that, even if assimilation is desirable, not everyone can assimilate and make it. Leonard Dinnerstein and Frederic Cople Jaher point out: "Although popular rhetoric [has] glorified the country as a melting pot of different peoples, in actuality this has meant melting diversity into conformity with Anglo-Saxon characteristics. Those unable or unwilling to accomplish the transformation have suffered varying degrees of abuse and ostracism because middle class America demands conformity before it gives acceptance."[21] Those with physical features and cultures defined as most unlike Anglo-Saxons face the greatest "abuse and ostracism."[22]

Color-blind arguments ultimately perpetuate the status quo. Ignoring race or the centrality of race enables those with power (whites) to maintain the facade of a meritocracy. In short, if race and racism as significant social factors are ignored, then privilege and power appear to be earned or merited. Likewise, failure to make it can be dismissed as an individual failing. Attention is diverted from institutional and individual racism, and once again people of color are told to change their culture, physical features, or attitude.[23] Michael Eric Dyson writes: "The goal should not be to transcend race, but to transcend the biased meanings associated with race. Ironically, the very attempt to transcend race by denying its presence reinforces its power to influence perceptions because it gains strength in secrecy."[24] Moreover, a color-blind perspective ignores the need for racial identification in a society in which race matters. To claim an identity as a human is a luxury and a privilege shared by those who do not suffer as a result of existing racial categories.

In life, conceptions of the color line are not so easily kept apart. Individuals may vacillate among perspectives, incorporating more than one into their thinking at any given moment. If we believe that race is essential and inherent to individuals, then race is a simple concept: we either have a particular gene or we don't. Social inequalities and cultures are explained as factors of heredity, and community boundaries can be established with the help of a DNA test. If we understand race as a social construction, the outcome of power struggles, then race becomes central to explanations of social injustice. Differing values assigned to human bodies are acknowledged as important and institutionalized. If we believe that race doesn't matter or exist, then social inequalities can be ignored or explained by factors other than race. Differences are ignored, denied, or discounted in an effort to build a universal human community of sameness or to justify injustice.

Multiracial family members occupy a unique place in our racialized society. Whether by birth, adoption, or marriage, they are at some point challenged to think about race in their relationships with themselves and others. The way in which many of them articulate race reflects both the pervasiveness and strength of racial essentialism and color-blind thinking. The complexities of race cause many family members to shift perspective. They envision and call on competing color lines as they attempt to understand their lives, sense of community(ies), identity(ies), and politics.

Three primary themes run through this book: the hurtfulness (and, for whites, the invisibility) of whiteness and racism; the lack of language available to describe multiracial experiences in positive terms; and the individual and institutional demands constantly placed on multiracial family members to conform to a racially divided (and racist) system. These demands reflect the pervasiveness of essentialist thinking in the United States. By examining the experiences and perspectives of multiracial family members, we can begin to consider race in a more sophisticated and progressive way—to see how race is constructed in and central to daily life.

## Tripping on the Color Line

**tripping** (trip-ping), v.i. [trip, trippin, tripped out]
1. physical and emotional response to a mind-blowing
idea or experience. 2. a. having fun at someone else's
expense; b. overreacting; presenting oneself in an inappropriate manner. 3. a stumbling over words; mis-
speaking or stuttering. b. stumbling or falling physically.
SYN.—trip, a journey.

The closer individuals live to the color line, the more often
they are forced to contend with the changing dynamics of
race. Multiracial family members live so close to the line—
it weaves through their families—that they are daily con
tending with the ambiguities and contradictions of race.
People who spend their leisure and family time in single-race
interactions often take racial categories for granted. They may
think of race as a simple concept. Those individuals who live
close to the line, however, know that race is anything but
simple. They are challenged to question what it means to be
black or white. On a day-to-day level, race can get very confusing. They stumble, fumble, act inappropriately, and sometimes feel blown away. They may trip in all kinds of ways.
Race itself is a trip, a journey. They travel through hardship,
anger, solidarity, unity, hostility, terror, growth, happiness,
fear, and uncertainty. Sometimes elusive, always present, race
is a social construct that guides the journey of human growth
and community. My hope is that, as we travel through our
racialized world, we will all think about the racial picture
we envision and create and all look into our own suitcases
to discover what we are adding to more than five centuries
worth of racial baggage. This book is my suitcase of sorts.
It is my attempt to introduce the world of race through the
eyes of multiracial family members—perspectives that may

help us all to rethink the ways in which all Americans trip on race.

**Tripping (trip-ping) 1. physical and emotional response to a mind-blowing idea or experience**

In *Crossing the Color Line,* Maureen Reddy talks about her "mind-blowing" discovery of racism in society through her interracial marriage. "Something inside her snapped" one day when she and her husband were attempting to rent a motel room; she physically attacked a racist and antagonistic motel clerk.[25] At other times she verbally assaulted overt racists. She explains, "I started to feel like a maniac, unable to control myself and my new-found propensity for violence, a sort of Dr. Jekyll and Ms. Hyde for the twentieth century."[26] During the sixties we might have said that her late-in-life discovery of racism was making her trip, that these incidents were blowing her mind.

In my travels among multiracial families I have come across many white interracial parents and partners who share Reddy's sense of tripping. Interracially married whites who grew up in single-race families and segregated neighborhoods had world views that were radically challenged once they became involved with their black partners. Whites, more than other multiracial family members, spoke of being blown away by racism because they were unprepared for the terror and hurt. As whites, they had learned to expect certain privileges—what they considered fair and just practices in society. But once they joined an interracial family, many discovered that the world is neither fair, just, nor equal. The privileges most whites take for granted become glaringly visible.

I met Candace through an ad I placed in the *Interracial Family Network Newsletter,* based in Evanston, Illinois. She explained that she and her husband had been married since the early seventies and had five grown, successful children. Through more than three hours of tape-recorded interviews and several other meetings, she unfolded her life story. Discussing her experiences as a blond-haired, blue-eyed woman, Candace explained why she and other interracially married whites trip out when they discover racism: "As whites, when we walk out, we're just assuming everyone will accept us. And as an interracial couple, you suddenly realize they don't, and you've never had these experiences before, and they're ugly and traumatic, and they'll shock you."

Barbara, a white interracially married librarian in a southern suburb of Chicago, was introduced to me through a mutual friend. She and I met a couple of times in her office. With my tape recorder on the desk, she began to recall her more than twenty-five years in a multiracial family. One particular incident stood out in her mind as the defining moment when racist actions blew her mind and forced her to rethink all she had been taught in her working-class Polish Catholic upbringing. One sunny day, she and her husband were making the rounds of various bookstores. On their way home, the police began harassing them for no apparent reason:

> Suddenly they are out of the squad, have him against the wall, have their guns drawn, the other cop has got me, and they were just standing there laughing. And I didn't know any better, so I just burst into tears and said, "What the hell are you doing?" I just started crying and said, "Why are you doing this to us?" And when we got to the El stop, my husband was shaking; we got on the train, and tears just streamed down his face. I thought to myself, "What kind of world is this where it's okay for the cops to do whatever they want to and treat you like dirt?"

Barbara was forced to question her taken-for-granted understandings of fair, just, and equal treatment for all. She
recalled this period of her life as "entering a nightmare."
Rather than receiving the privileges granted to people with
white skin, she now recognizes and faces the terror of whiteness—something few whites ever experience.[27] A color-blind
perspective is no longer possible.

**Tripping (trip-ping) 2. a. stumbling over words; mis-
speaking or stuttering. b. stumbling or falling,
physically**

Another way in which we trip on the color line is
through our language. We have both competing words and
a lack of words to describe race identities and racial experiences, particularly when it comes to multiracialism. Think
about all the terms for multiracialism: multiracial, mixed
race, biracial, mulatto, interracial, half black, half white, half
breed, half caste, half and half, multiethnic, blendo, vanilla
swirl, chocolate swirl, black and white, African American
and Caucasian, human, zebra, Oreo, sellout, race traitor, yellow boy, red boy, wannabe, white trash, jungle fever,
crossover, Cablinasian, new people, beige warriors, gray
ladies, wiggers.[28] Some terms are meant to be sensitive, others meant to hurt. All are meant to include every person
somewhere in the nation's racial classification system.

Because they do not quite fit into the historically created,
officially named, and socially recognized categories, members of multiracial families are constantly fighting to identify themselves for themselves. A difficulty they face is the
lack of language available to address their experiences. For
example, a few years ago I was invited to speak at Chicago's
Expo for Today's Black Woman as a member of a panel
exploring multiracialism. The panel consisted of three multiracial women and me. The moderator, a well-known

author, asked each panel member to "tell us a bit about your background and how you identify racially."

One woman replied, "My father is white; my mother is black. I grew up with my mother, was not raised to think of myself as multiracial, and so I am black. I do not identify myself as anything other than black."

Another responded, "I cannot deny either one of my parents. They both raised me, and I am here because of them. I identify as multiracial."

Assuming that I had been invited to speak about racial categories in the U.S. census, I had not formulated a response to this question. I began to babble: "Well, it's very complex. Because of my experiences, I no longer claim a white identity."

With an edge in her voice, the moderator asked, "I don't understand. Then what identity do you claim?"

Knowing that the audience of a hundred or so people was likewise baffled by my response I said, "Well, racial identities are formed in large part through our experiences. As an interracially married woman, my experiences are vastly different from other white women. Things like being seated in the back of restaurants, being denied loans, being steered out of white neighborhoods when we search for housing, being pulled over for no reason, and facing hostility from racist whites are experiences most whites never contend with. Because of my experiences, I no longer take white privilege for granted, and in some cases I am no longer seen as white by other whites."

She pressed, "So what identity do you claim?"

I began struggling for words and found only what seemed to be a confused cop-out: "Well, that's the problem; there is no language to describe it. There is no other racial identity for me to claim. I am still working on that."

A young man in the audience said, "Well, then just say you're black."

I thought for a moment. I was not raised in a black community and did not participate in black culture. I do not want to be disrespectful to those who suffer racist abuse, and I don't want to make cultural claims to which I am not entitled. I recognize that I am granted many privileges based on my skin color. I replied, "People will think I'm a bit nuts. That's not an option in this society." Identities are expressions of our experiences mediated by language. Because essentialist thinking and language is so prevalent, many multiracial family members do not have a language to express various identities. Instead, we find ourselves bound by the color line.

Marie P. P. Root, a pioneer in writing about the lives of multiracial Americans, suggests that the nation's racial vocabulary continues to create "border markers" or "rigid reflections upon our history of race relations and racial classifications."[29] In other words, as we begin to challenge traditional understandings of race, we must create a new language lest we reproduce the same old ideology. The language used in the United States is couched in a history of dichotomous western thinking: people are categorized as belonging in *either* one group *or* the other.[30] Individuals are expected to be either gay or straight, abled or disabled, black or white, male or female; there is no room for in between.[31] Individuals who do not comfortably fit into preset categories face ridicule and rejection. A few years ago Saturday Night Live featured a skit about Pat, who had a gender-ambiguous appearance and name. In various situations people attempted to figure out if Pat was male or female; but Pat continually defied gender classification and thus got big laughs from the audience. Many will argue that it is human nature to categorize. By placing the world into categories we save time and energy and feel safer. Fair enough. But why are particular distinctions made and how does power become central to our systems of categorizing human beings? Categories, like differences, are not inherently problematic. Many dichotomous categories exist in life. The difficulties emerge when one side of the dichotomy has more power than the other. Multiracial family members who refuse or defy traditional racial categories are constantly asked to explain and defend their thoughts and actions. They are often told that they can't be mixed or asked, "How is that possible?" and pitied with comments such as "It must be so hard to be mixed" or "I couldn't see myself in an interracial relationship."

Some multiracial family members do claim either a black or a white identity from time to time and even for extended periods.[32] Most move in and out of various racial identities, something that has been called "traveling."[33] Traveling is not well tolerated in a society built on a racial hierarchy with a defined color line. It undermines the strength of what many consider the natural and unchanging color line. The language used to describe people who travel is generally negative: sellout, wannabe, mixed up. Interacting and being comfortable with both sides seems to indicate confusion, weak self-esteem, and a lack of firm politics. Multiracial family members must travel between and within single-race categories and communities; after all, that is how society is set up. The lack of positive language to describe their experiences means that they are continually challenged to create their own language of description.[34]

How multiracial family members describe themselves depends largely on age, physical features, class, family structure, neighborhood, larger racial politics, our own ideas about social justice, educational level, peer group, and other experiences within a racially divided and racist society. What they call themselves is not arbitrary or static. Much thought goes into this naming. Each person I interviewed gave specific reasons for the labels they used to describe themselves. Some named themselves publicly and politically as black and identified themselves in private in ways that reflect the complexity of racial experiences.[35] Others attempted to find a word or words that would describe their racial identity. For instance, Andrea, a twenty-four-year-old biracial lesbian recalled her painful childhood in a predominantly white section of the Bronx. She was the youngest child of an Irish American mother and the only biracial sibling (her brothers and sisters are white). She never knew her biological father and had little contact with black Americans. One day she came home from school crying because other children had called her a nigger. Without emotion her mother responded, "You're not, so don't worry about it." From that day on, Andrea felt she had no support in her daily struggle as the only child of color in a white Catholic grade school. She explained why she now calls herself biracial rather than interracial, multiracial, or mixed: "With all the animosity I was seeing in my family and the world around me, *inter* implies that there is a meshing and a coupling, and I didn't see a whole lot of that. For me there's definitely two races in existence. I wanted a term that would define both races without having what I perceive to be a charade."

Andrea's chosen label signifies the racial world—split, contentious, and unequal. She makes a statement about the racial divisions she has experienced in life. The reason she cites for claiming a biracial identity is the same reason that many others cite for *not* calling themselves and their families biracial. Silvia, a twenty-nine-year-old woman who grew up with a black father, a white mother, and multiracial siblings in a predominantly black section of Washington, D.C., prefers to call herself mixed. Because she has large, bright-blue eyes and light brown hair, she has to tell people she is mixed, or many assume she is white. Silvia participated in one of my first interviews. At the time I had not figured out what language I was comfortable using; the term I had heard most often was biracial. Near the end of the interview she said, "Biracial sounds half and half rather than mixed, which is all mixed up." Swirling her hands in the air, she said, "In me it really is all mixed. I suppose this is really esoteric, but it's like that with me." After this interview I began to listen to how people described themselves. I used their own terms during interviews and asked each person to explain how he or she had decided what label to choose.

Interracial parents and partners had a particularly difficult time finding language to describe their experiences and racial identities. Often arguments made by and for the recognition of multiracial experiences draw on the idea that individuals possess two or more heritages.[36] Because they cannot claim parents of different heritages, however, interracially married people are left to defend and describe their own shifting identities within a language that connotes race as a biological construct. Self-descriptions may be laced with qualifications and default into either essentialist language or color-blind rhetoric. For instance, Lionel, a forty-two-year-old black interracially married father living in a middle class neighborhood in Montclair, New Jersey, is careful to preface how he identifies racially: "I think because of my experiences, although I am not mixed race, I can identify to some degree with a mixed-race person." Likewise, Jane, a sixty-five-year-old white woman living in a poor, predominantly black neighborhood on Chicago's South Side can "identify to some degree." Now widowed, she lives in the same house she and her black husband purchased in the 1950s and in which they raised their three children. She, too, grounds her identity in her experiences and is careful about the wording she chooses to describe herself: "I identify as multiethnic because I feel that in terms of environment I've become multiethnic. I don't want to say multiracial because race involves, or is generally considered to involve, genetic inheritance. I have lived in a black neighborhood for more years than I lived in a white neighborhood—ever since I was married. My experiences are much different than the experiences of white families." Both Lionel and Jane feel the need to qualify their claimed identity in a society that has historically thought of race in biological terms—and continues to do so.

Like Jane, who claims a multiethnic identity, others suggest that we should change our language. Instead of talking about race, they believe we should talk about ethnicity, arguing that the concept allows us to account for our lived and claimed experiences rather than present a false sense of identity based solely on appearance. I prefer to use the word *race* when referring to the historically, politically, culturally, economically, and socially created categories used to determine the distribution of resources and power. In short, I prefer to challenge hurtful ideologies head on, believing that by switching our language from race to ethnicity, we allow racial myths to continue. Moreover, problems are not solved by ignoring them. If we want to deal with all the social and personal implications of race, we must begin a dialogue. The inequalities and injustices are too glaring to ignore. In fact, much of what multiracial family members bring to traditional race debates is a desire to talk openly about racial issues.

Throughout this book I most often rely on the terms *multiracial, interracial, black,* and *white* rather than *Caucasian, European American,* and *African American.* Not all black people consider themselves African American; some prefer Caribbean American, and many are Latinos. The term *European American* does not address the invisibility and terror of institutionalized white supremacy, nor does it speak to the

privileges granted to whites in the United States. Moreover, the terms *African American* and *European American*
(or *Caucasian*) are often saved for mixed crowds. Race, as the
construction of inequality, is anything but polite. Arguments can be made in many directions about the choice of
terms, but I want to highlight *black* and *white* as separate
and unequal categories. (When referring to individuals whom
I have spoken with, I do use their own preferred terms.) Silvia, the woman who prefers to be called mixed, says it best:
"I like the terms *black* and *white* because they are both
equally impossible. Just as there are no coal-black people,
there are no snow-white people either. And so you can see
they've been constructed to mean what they mean."

> *Tripping* **(trip-ping) 3. a. having fun at someone else's**
> **expense; b. overreacting; presenting oneself in an**
> **inappropriate manner**

Skin color and physical features identify and locate
people in a racially divided nation. Single-race people (those
who comfortably claim one racial identity and group) may
feel confusion, anger, skepticism, concern, pity, hostility,
curiosity, or superiority when they meet someone who does
not seem to fit neatly into a preset racial category. The way
in which they react to members of multiracial families
highlights the investment or comfort they have in existing
racial categories.

Multiracial people are regularly asked, "What are you?"
Those with light skin and European features are often challenged when they claim a black or multiracial identity. Silvia, with her blue eyes, has faced this situation many times:
"The thing about my blue eyes, I tell people that I'm mixed
and they don't believe me and insist that I'm wrong, which
pisses me off more than anything. I say, 'I'm mixed; my
father's black.' And they go, 'No, you're not.'" She laughs

as she recalls their boldness. " 'Yes I am!' I say. Then they say, 'But you have blue eyes.' And I say, 'I don't care what color my eyes are; I'm mixed!' " Still chuckling, she notes that whites tend to have this reaction more than blacks do: "Black people will usually say, 'Oh yeah, I can see it in your lips or hips.' They accept what I am saying. Whites are more likely to argue." With power, privilege, and identity at stake, combined with a general lack of awareness, whites argue with her. But a wide range of appearances in black families helps blacks "see it."

Interracially married people and members of multiracial families who appear to be single race are often assigned to a category and then treated accordingly. All kinds of decisions must be made by multiracial family members about how to respond to essentialist assumptions and demands. There is a pervasive feeling among multiracial family members that most people just don't get it. Instead of considering the color line as a problem, essentialist thinkers often see members of multiracial families as the problem, the mistake. Most people who think in essentialist terms have not had experiences that challenge traditional "stick with your own" racial thinking. Members of multiracial families learn that racial identities are far from static. Brothers and sisters may identify differently, and their identities change over time.[37] The identities they claim and the life experiences they highlight as important change depending on the group they are with, their mood, the larger political and racial climate, their age, and many other factors. Others may decide that multiracial family members are wishy-washy, lack self-esteem, and need therapy. On the contrary, many family members talk about being well grounded and having matured in their understandings of race precisely because of their multiracial experiences. Granted, this can be a difficult concept for people who do not live it to understand. Thus, many multiracial family members have stopped trying to explain or defend themselves and instead "trip on," or have fun at the expense of, people who cling to a belief that the color line is natural and normal and crossing the color line is pathological.

Many multiracial family members recall times when they have tripped on essentialist thinkers as a way to force a rethinking of racial paradigms. For instance, Kimberly, a twenty-five-year-old mixed-race woman living in Manhattan, spoke in detail about growing up in Brooklyn and attending a racially divided Manhattan high school. She and her sister were raised for several years by her Irish American paternal grandparents. As children, the girls were chastised by their parents and grandparents if they did not speak "proper" English; and Kimberly was taunted by many black students who insisted that she was trying to be white. As a person with racially ambiguous features, she receives many questions from strangers. Because she is tired of hearing the same questions and comments from people, she often chooses to trip instead of explaining and defending herself. "People come up to me and they'll say, 'Do you get confused between being black and white?' I say, 'Well, yeah, you know, some mornings I wake up with this craving for fried chicken, and other mornings I just can't get the beat, I start dancing and can't get the beat.' I want them to see how narrow-minded they're being. What do you think? One day I like fried chicken, and the next I don't? It's not like that."

Each time I give a talk about multiracialism, I include Kimberly's wonderful rebuttal. Audiences pause for a moment and then laugh. By tripping, Kimberly challenges others to think differently about race—to think about their own essentialist assumptions. When they discover the topic of my research, writings, and talks, people who don't know me often want to know why I'm interested in studying multiracialism. I know what they really want to know: "You look white, so why are you studying this? Are you interracially married or multiracial or have you transracially adopted a child?" They need to put me into a category so they can get a handle on our relationship to each other. Since I have been faced with a variety of questions over the years, I sometimes take the opportunity to trip. One evening I was eating with a group of people. A white woman I had just met began inquiring about my work. "What caused you to choose that topic?" she inquired loudly.

"I think we can learn a lot about race by listening to the experiences of multiracial family members," I said, knowing I was not answering the question she was really asking.

She pushed on, determined to get to the root of it all: "Yes, but why did *you* choose this topic?"

At this point I was inwardly chuckling because while she was practiced at the art of rudeness, I was practiced at the art of evasion—not because I deny my racial location or want to pass but because quick answers don't always make people think. Moreover, one answer on my part often leads to twenty more personal and probing questions. I responded, "Like all things sociologists study, it's a convergence of intellectual, social, and personal interests." I intentionally turned away to join another conversation. Without a pause she asked her next question. From across the table, she burst out with "Well, do you come from a multiracial family?" I pretended not to hear her outburst, although it gave me great enjoyment to know that she was now forced to bask in the unknown. Afterwards, a friend of mine laughed heartily and asked, "Why'd you have to trip on her like that?" Certainly, I could have just given this woman the information she wanted in her first question, but I was in a mood to trip. I didn't feel like explaining or defending myself. I wanted to relax, and I hoped that the lack of an answer might cause her to think about race for longer than a New York minute, something whites aren't often asked to do.

## Tripping (trip-ping) SYN.—trip, a journey

In this book we journey back and forth, through and around the color line, and in the process we will trip and stumble. We will trip on essentialist thinkers, we will trip over the language, we will explore the many ways race is "really tripped out," and, yes, we will go on a sometimes mind-blowing trip through the racial world as seen through the eyes of multiracial family members.

### Overview

Chapter 1 explores the ways in which discrimination directed at interracial couples challenges them to rethink race, racism, their own racial identities, and their connection to race-based communities. Multiracial family members, by their very existence, threaten essentialist and racist thinking and thus endanger the color line. The discrimination and hostility directed toward multiracial families reflect continuing efforts to maintain the line. If that line were in fact genetically drawn, if race were essential, then multiracial family members would pose no threat to the racial system because they would not exist.

Chapter 2 explores how institutional racism in the housing market creates and maintains a color line. Specifically, the connection between housing and other issues such as identity, social status, educational opportunities, and friendship networks strengthens ideas about racial essentialism. In short, while segregation and inequality in the housing market are socially created, they appear to have essentialist underpinnings. The appearance of housing segregation as a natural division has major ramifications for multiracial families who are attempting to fit their racially mixed households into a racially divided and racist housing market. Their experiences highlight the way in which we all "do" race and create the color line while negotiating the institutionally and individually created color line.

Chapter 3 shows how multiracial family members are seen as racially ambiguous because of either physical appearance, politics, or familial relations. The ways in which individuals think about race and their own racial identity inform how they respond and interact with others. Encounters with racially ambiguous people can cause some essentialist thinkers to question their own racial identity. Thus, the chapter considers how the color line is contested and shaped in the course of daily interactions.

Chapter 4 explores how racial thinking and identities are shaped in the context of organizing, creating networks, and building community. In particular, it focuses on two political hotbeds: census categories and transracial adoption debates. Underlying much of the discussion is an essentialist belief that humans can and should fit into prescribed racial categories. When multiracial family members enter the debates, they bring experiences that challenge traditional and essentialist racial categories and the politics developed around them. Unfortunately, some members of multiracial families have begun making essentialist-based claims about *the* multiracial community. A struggle against racial injustice that draws on essentialism risks reproducing and strengthening injustice. Instead, the struggle must include an understanding that race is socially constructed—that is, a conscious understanding of the ways we "do" race during daily interactions, community building, political choices, and self-identification. Ultimately, this book explores the ways in which multiracial family members' identities, politics, and communities both shape and are shaped by the color line.

# 1

## *Discovering*

## *Racial*

## *Borders*

The closer individuals live to the color line and the more disadvantaged they are by it, the more they find themselves reflecting on and reformulating racial thinking. Multiracial family members spend a great deal of time talking, thinking, and theorizing about race. They must. As visible indicators that the color line has been breached, they become lightning rods for racial thoughts, actions, and discussions. At one extreme, they stand as symbolic proof that race no longer matters in society. Some believe that Gunnar Myrdal was right: given enough time, all groups can be absorbed into mainstream culture.[1] The unspoken text is "if blacks and whites are intermarrying, then race must not matter as much anymore." At the other extreme, multiracial family members represent decline, sin, and tragedy. We threaten "the assumption of stable, pure, racial identities," the existence of an essentialist color line.[2]

Unlike multiracial and transracially adopted people who grow up across the color line, interracially married people often grow up in single-race families and communities, learn about themselves and the world through a single-race lens, and later make the decision to cross the color line. Their decision-making processes and the reactions of others show that the color line is internalized and central to human thought, action, and larger social institutions. As these individuals confront the expressed curiosity and hostility of others, they begin to question earlier understandings of race. They begin to think about and "do" race differently. Because multiracial family members visibly challenge race in the United States, their own racial identities and politics cannot be taken for granted.

Throughout history, individuals invested in maintaining the color line have patrolled the line on both sides, albeit for different and often opposing reasons. Whites patrol to protect privilege, blacks as they struggle for liberation. Borders created to protect resources such as goods and power are kept in place by laws, language, cultural norms, images, and individual actions as well as by interlocking with other borders. Many borders exist, and each has a unique history laden with power struggles. Think about some of them: national, religious, political, sexual, gender, racial. People are raised to understand their world through borders. They are taught from an early age to know where borders exist and the consequences for attempting to cross them. For instance, a boy is chastised for wanting to wear a dress or play with dolls while a girl is chastised for wanting to play football. We learn to look for specific indicators, we learn the boundaries, in the process of categorizing. Later we learn about the power associated with the categories. The greater the power imbalance, the greater the consequences. According to Constance Perin, "boundaries are the main characteristic of any category, and universally they are freighted with significance. . . . boundaries are sources of power. . . . without boundaries, categories have no force."[3] As when touching a hot stove, we learn where the boundaries are and avoid getting too close. We curtail our behaviors, thoughts, and desires so as not to get burned. By doing and seeing what is considered racially appropriate, we reinforce the strength of the categories and build borders.

A recent study of racial recognition in the United States reports that children as young as three years old begin recognizing skin color differences.[4] While the issue of power may not be readily apparent to them, they do learn to make distinctions based on societal definitions of *difference*. Barbara Katz Rothman recalls a trip to New Zealand, where she attended a Maori ceremony and discovered that she couldn't tell "who's Maori by looking." When she shared this observation with a white New Zealand acquaintance, that person was confused. Wasn't it obvious? Rothman writes, "Seeing race is always about discriminating, a discerning, trained eye recognizing the 'essential' or defining characteristic(s) in the individual that confer(s) racial categorization."[5] After learning to see race, we then naturalize the categories, internalize the borders, and assume the differences to be essential. In turn, we see ourselves through categories.

Borders give each person a sense of ourselves in the world; they help us know where we fit, what our status is, and who our people are. They teach us what is significant in society. The borders maintain the shape of the category and are meant to stop one category from leaking into the next. Grace Elizabeth Hale notes, "The act of trying to clarify the boundary between white and black reveal[s] the fluidity of the color line."[6] When borders are crossed, essentialist explanations are threatened. Ultimately, borders maintain the color line and the strength of race by making race appear natural.

## Racial Borders

Racial borders include the contested, patrolled, and often hostile spaces near the color line. Historical creations, borders have become institutionalized and internalized. They exist in how society is structured as well as in how individuals learn to think about and act on race. Since Europeans first attempted to institute their racialized system in the New World, race has been contested. Only recently, however, (since the civil rights movement—specifically, the 1967 Supreme Court ruling against anti-miscegenation laws) have large numbers of people recognized these borders and overtly contested them.[7] At other times, whites have not tolerated such identification, nor have blacks and other people of color struggling for a unified front against a white supremacist system necessarily desired it.[8]

During slavery and Reconstruction, blacks were denied any form of legitimized power and were forced to struggle for physical survival. Through legal and extralegal forms of physical and psychological violence, whites imposed a racist system.[9] Any perceived transgression against the white supremacist system—against the imposed color line—was met with violence or death, a means that allowed whites to create a sense of unity. In *Making Whiteness*, Grace Elizabeth Hale documents the way in which lynchings and lynching narratives created "white unity within the nation as well as the region."[10] Because of the terror created by violence, people defined as black and thus as potential slaves began to suppress cultural and linguistic differences and build their own basis for unity; the color line began to be patrolled on both sides.[11] Slaves who were coerced or who chose to interact with whites in ways that threatened slave unity faced sanctions from other slaves. In *Mixed Blood*, Paul Spikard reports that "slaves frequently marked off a woman who had chosen the role of concubine and refused to have more than perfunctory dealings with her."[12] In short, as whites were creating a system in which all privileges were bestowed on whites at the expense of blacks, blacks were unifying in a struggle for survival and liberation.

By the 1950s, close to ninety years after the signing of the Emancipation Proclamation, black communities had mobilized into the civil rights movement. As they began claiming state-legitimized power, white lawmakers were forced to retreat from the most overt forms of discrimination; white privilege became more covert, institutionalized, and invisible.[13] As an example, Manning Marable cites "educational apartheid."[14] He suggests that the United States no longer relies on overt racism to maintain white supremacy. The segregated and unequal housing market, coupled with the way in which schools are funded, maintains a separate and unequal system ensuring that black children from poor (often segregated) neighborhoods will not compete for college admission and jobs with their wealthier white counterparts. Removing opportunities for individuals to compete in a capitalist system is as effective as having a caste system that traps children in poverty.[15] This discrimination is part of how society functions.

People need not burn crosses for racism to persist; yet because racism has been institutionalized, many Americans don't see it. For instance, HBO recently featured interviews with young people from various racial and class backgrounds. The interviewer asked two African American teens if they had ever faced discrimination. The teens lived in a segregated, poor, and violent neighborhood and attended schools in which they were clearly denied an education comparable to that of their wealthier white peers. The teens said they had never been discriminated against. With institutional discrimination so apparent, why didn't these teens see it? According to bell hooks, they may feel the outcome of discrimination but are unable to articulate it: "Black people still feel the terror, still associate it with whiteness, but are rarely able to articulate the varied ways we are terrorized because it is easy to be silenced by accusations of reverse racism or by suggesting that black folks who talk about the ways we are terrorized by whites are merely evoking victimization to demand special treatment."[16] Moreover, discrimination is taught and thought of as something that happens between individuals. Perhaps in their segregated world these teens have not experienced overt racism from whites. In fact, it is possible that they have not interacted with whites at all. Thus, after hearing these teens report a lack of discrimination, wealthier white suburbanites feel reassured about their "earned" privilege. Reducing social, institutional, and systemic problems to an individual level allows whites to maintain the fallacy that white privilege does not exist, that race no longer really matters, and that we live in a meritocratic society. Meanwhile, the futures of white children are being protected and helped through systemic discrimination.[17] An invisible and institutionalized color line has largely replaced state-sanctioned chains, ropes, fire hoses, and overtly racist laws.[18]

Whites do not necessarily need to exercise individual effort to protect their racial privilege; the system takes care of it. Most of them (barring those involved in white supremacist groups) do not give race much conscious thought. When race arises as a factor, they often push it into the background without examining it. This lack of critical thought and denial of the significance of race may be a stronger border protecting the color line than any overt action is. For example, a student recently caught up with me in the hallway: "Hey, Professor Dalmage, I want to run something past you. The other morning I was sitting out on my porch, and I looked up and down the street and noticed that all the lawns were perfectly manicured except for two. These two just happen to belong to the only families of color on the block. One is a Spanish-speaking family, and the other from a Middle Eastern country." Although I did not know where this conversation was leading, I did know this student was someone who tried hard to understand himself as a privileged white male in society. "So I'm thinking," he continued, "what does this mean, you know, sociologically? I know what my neighbors are thinking. I've heard them talk. But I don't know how to interpret this. Is it just a different cultural norm, or maybe it's just that they don't have as much time because they have to work a lot or. . . ." His voice trailed off. Finally, he asked, "I don't know, am I a racist for even thinking this stuff?" His question exemplifies how racial borders play out in the context of a post–civil rights system of whiteness. Instead of exploring the context and meaning of perfectly manicured lawns among middle-class whites, he assumed that such lawns were the norm and questioned the deviant families of color. Moreover, questioning race on any level makes many whites fear they may be labeled as racist. Their fear silences both critical analysis and opportunities to explore the ways in which race is constructed. Without that exploration, they lose the opportunity to explore racism and white privilege critically.

Unfortunately, many whites are raised to believe that consciously acknowledging differences is both judgmental and racist. Those whites striving to be good liberals avoid any reference to race. They would point out a freckle on the side of someone's face before they would use race as an identifier. Most whites have been caught in a conversation like this:

White Person 1 asks, "What man are you talking about?"

White Person 2, referring to a black man, replies, "Oh, the guy that had on the blue pants and a striped shirt. He was about 5'11", has a mustache, drives a Honda. He just left here two minutes ago."

And on it goes. In many cases, the man in question may have been the only black man to leave. Three words would have clarified the initial question: "the black man." But the goal here is to ignore references to race. I find such conversations terribly frustrating and often cut to the chase when I see the road we're traveling: "Was he white or black?" Often, the response will be poorly acted shock: "Oh, well, he's black, yeah." In short, beyond institutional mechanisms the color line is protected by borders that exist in the minds of many whites. Like my student, they become afraid to talk and think critically about race. Moreover, they equate race with people of color, assuming that "white" is the unquestioned, invisible, and raceless norm. Whites learn that there is no good or proper way to talk about race. Silence and whispers become the modus operandi. This silence protects whiteness. If race isn't discussed, then racism needn't be acknowledged or addressed. Discussions of race, particularly with people of color, make it clear to whites that others are watching and analyzing their whiteness.[19] Institutions, social norms, silence, and a lack of critical thought maintain the color line's white advantages.

### Borderism

To live near the color line, in the space Gloria Anzaldúa calls the borderlands, means to contend constantly with what I call borderism.[20] Borderism is a unique form of discrimination faced by those who cross the color line, do not stick with their own, or attempt to claim membership (or are placed by others) in more than one racial group. Like racism, borderism is central to American society. It is a product of a racist system yet comes from both sides. The manner in which people react to individuals who cross the color line highlights the investment, the sense of solidarity, and perhaps the comfort these observers have with existing categories. Perhaps most important, the reaction shows the wide acceptance of racial essentialism as the explanation for the color line. When the color line is crossed, the idea of immutable, biologically based racial categories is threatened. The individual who has crossed the line must be explained away or punished so that essentialist categories can remain in place. Ironically, if race were natural and essential, individuals would not have to engage in borderism. The act of borderism is one of the many ways in which individuals construct or "do" race.

Multiracial family members contend with borderism in many aspects of life. It is both part of the workings of larger institutions and the outcome of individual actions. When families are unable to find accepting places of worship and comfortable neighborhoods, they contend with examples of institutional borderism. A nefarious individual is not responsible for creating these situations. Rather, this borderism has developed in the context of a deeply racist and segregated society. Some borderism, however, does play out on an individual level and is meant to be hurtful. A family disowns a child for not sticking with his own. Peers tell a multiracial child that she is not black enough. An interracial couple is physically accosted in the street. Such borderism may stem from hostility, hatred, or feelings of betrayal and is grounded in ideas about how people ought to act. But it may also reveal concern. For example, before returning to graduate school I was working for a corporation that sent me to the Baltimore–Washington, D.C., area for a summer. It was a racially tense season. The Klan was active, hanging notices all over one town declaring it a "nigger-free zone." In another town white men killed a black man because he was walking with a white woman in a white neighborhood. When my husband, Philip, came to visit, we were cautious. One weekend went without incident until I dropped him off at the train station. We were talking when an elderly black woman walked up to Philip and scolded, "Get away from her; she's going to get you killed. You need to stick with your own." I believe she meant to be helpful to Philip. After all, another black man had just been killed. Nonetheless, these moments can be paralyzing. In such situations there is no way for me to say, "Please, my skin color belies my politics. I am likewise outraged and live with the fear of violence." For me to speak at these moments is to belittle the history of racial oppression and the fact that I do represent, in my physical being, the object and the symbol that has been used to justify so much oppression. Protecting white women's bodies has long been the justification for abusing and lynching thousands of black men and women.[21]

All members of multiracial families face borderism, although as individuals we face specific forms of discrimination based on our race, physical features, gender, and other socially significant markers. Borderism consists of three interacting components: *border patrolling*, discrimination that comes from both sides; *rebound racism*, faced by interracially married whites and white-looking members of multiracial families; and *intensified racism*, faced by interracially married blacks.[22] Each form is directed specifically at people who cross the color line. Although I address each as a discrete experience, in reality they are inextricably linked and are always grounded in a larger racist system. As a primary means of re-creating, reproducing, and clarifying the color line, borderism shows how individuals and institutions continue to create race.

### Border Patrolling

The belief that people ought to stick with their own is the driving force behind efforts to force individuals to follow prescribed racial rules. Border patrollers often think (without much critical analysis) that they can easily differentiate between insiders and outsiders. Once the patroller has determined a person's appropriate category, he or she will attempt to coerce that person into following the category's racial scripts. In *Race, Nation, Class: Ambiguous Identities,* Etienne Balibar and Immanuel Wallerstein observe that "people shoot each other every day over the question of labels. And yet, the very people who do so tend to deny that the issue is complex or puzzling or indeed anything but self-evident."[23] Border patrollers tend to take race and racial categories for granted. Whether grounding themselves in essentialist thinking or hoping to strengthen socially constructed racial categories, they believe they have the right and the need to patrol. Some people, especially whites, do not recognize the centrality and problems of the color line, as evinced in color-blind claims that "there is only one race: the human race" or "race doesn't really matter any more." Such thinking dismisses the terror and power of race in society. These individuals may patrol without being aware of doing so. In contrast, blacks generally see patrolling the border as both problematic and necessary.

While border patrolling from either side may be scary, hurtful, or annoying, we must recognize that blacks and whites are situated differently. The color line was imposed by whites, who now have institutional means for maintaining their power; in contrast, blacks must consciously and actively struggle for liberation. Repeatedly, people in multiracial families have told me, "The one thing that David Duke and Louis Farrakhan agree on is that we should not exist." What is not analyzed are the different historical legacies that bring both men to the same conclusion. The only form of borderism in which blacks engage is border patrolling, although they can act on prejudicial feelings and discriminate. After centuries of systemic control, only whites can be racist. As Joe Feagin and Hernán Vera explain, "black racism would require not only a widely accepted racist ideology directed at whites, but also the power to systematically exclude whites from opportunities and rewards in major economic, cultural, and political institutions."[24] White and black border patrollers may both dislike interracial couples and multiracial families, but their dislike comes from different historical and social perspectives. Moreover, border patrolling tends to take place intraracially: whites patrol whites, and blacks patrol black and multiracial people.

White Border Patrolling. Despite the institutional mechanisms in place to safeguard whiteness, many whites feel both the right and the obligation to act out against interracial couples. If a white person wants to maintain a sense of racial superiority, then he or she must attempt to locate motives and explain the actions of the white partner in the interracial couple. A white person who crosses the color line threatens the assumption that racial superiority is essential to whites. The interracially involved white person is thus often recategorized as inherently flawed—as "polluted."[25] In this way, racist and essentialist thinking remains unchallenged.

Frequently white families disown a relative who marries a person of color, but several people have told me that their families accepted them again once their children were born. The need to disown demonstrates the desire to maintain the facade of a pure white family.[26] By the time children are born, however, extended family members have had time to shift their racial thinking. Some grant acceptance by making an exception to the "rule," others by claiming to be color blind. Neither form of racial thinking, however, challenges the color line or white supremacy. In fact, both can be painful for the multiracial family members, who may face unending racist compliments such as "I'll always think of you as white."

The myth of purity is maintained by controlling white women's wombs. Thus, white women are patrolled more harshly than white men are. The regulations women face have not always been overtly displayed but have developed within the culture's conception of the *family ethic*, an ideal extant since the arrival of the early settlers that has influenced perceptions of proper work and home roles for white, middle-class family members.[27] The proper family should have a male breadwinner and patriarch and a female who makes her husband and obedient children her life's central work. According to Mimi Abramowitz, the family ethic "has made [women] the guardians of family and community morality, expected them to remain pious and chaste and to tame male sexuality, and defined them as weak and in need of male protection and control."[28] Ultimately, the family ethic has kept white women under the control of white men. In *Whiteness Visible: The Meaning of Whiteness in American Literature and Culture*, Valerie Babb notes that images depicting white women as helpless and in need of white men's protection grew against a backdrop of a developing patriarchy. White women faced particularly harsh regulations because the "loss of sexual purity through intercourse with other races endangers visible race difference, a key driving force behind an ideology of whiteness that gives political, economic, and social advantage to those with 'appropriate' race lineage."[29] The myth of white racial purity required white women to give birth to the offspring of white men—and only white men. Unfortunately, many white women have played active roles in maintaining this myth of purity. For instance, in 1897 one wrote: "If it takes lynching to protect women's dearest possession from drunken, ravening beasts, then I say lynch a thousand a week if it becomes necessary."[30] Today many white women who give birth to children of color give them up for adoption, fearing that as mothers of children of color they will become pariahs in their families and society at large.[31] Such complicity has worked to strengthen the color line and white-supremacist abuses.

It has been argued that white women should be protected because they are the gatekeepers of racial purity.[32] Any white woman who would trade in her white privilege and connections to white male power must be dismissed as unnaturally bad and bizarre. Julie, a white mother recently divorced from her black husband, has contended with white border patrolling and its underlying images. One incident (although not the only one) occurred while she was on a date with a white physician:

> He asked to see a picture of my daughter. I handed it to him. He was very clever; he asked, "Is her dad from the U.S.?"
>
> I think he was praying her dad was Spanish, and he could deal with that, anything but black. I could tell it bothered him, so I said, "Listen, I can see by the look on your face that there is obviously a problem here, so why don't we just talk about it right now."
>
> He said, "You want to know the truth? Well, I have a real problem with the fact that you slept with a black man." Then he went on with the whole, "You're such a pretty and intelligent woman; why would you marry a black man?"

Her date was drawing on the interlocking imagery of race and sex and what it means to be a good white woman. In his attempt to explain away Julie's behavior, he searched for motives, implying that only unattractive, unintelligent white women sleep with and marry black men. Further, the fact that she slept with a black man removed her eligibility as a white woman. She is assumed to be fundamentally and essentially changed. Perhaps he feared that his white purity would be contaminated with blackness through this bad white woman. Perhaps he felt threatened because he could not immediately detect her racial flaw. He may have begun to discover the mutability of race, which could undermine his own sense of racial superiority. While all people of color face some form of racist imagery in a white racist society, Julie notes the centrality and power given to racist images directed specifically against black people and interracially involved whites and blacks: "I think he was praying her dad was Spanish, and he could deal with that, anything but black."

Black men are seen "as a constant threat" to patriarchal whiteness.[33] Abby Ferber writes: "A photograph of a white woman with an Asian American man, for example, does not have the same symbolic power. The image of interracial sexuality between a white woman and a black man is pregnant with meaning in the American imagery. Powerful enough to serve as a symbol of all interracial sexuality."[34] White women who enter into interracial relationships with black men are often treated as aberrant, misguided white trash who are in this relationship solely for sex or rebellion. Barbara gained forty pounds because she "got tired of being mistaken for a prostitute." She explains, "It's assumed that the only reason you're involved in the relationship is because you're sexually depraved . . . that you've got to be the dregs of society to get involved or you want to hurt somebody." Women may be explained away as money or status seekers.[35] Often when we are out, people will ask Philip what he does for work. After learning he's an attorney, they don't bother to ask me what I do. This could be a gender issue; in a patriarchal world men are seen as the subjects, women the objects. But I often wonder how much it has do with assumptions about uncovering the motive behind our relationship—that I have traded my white status for his occupational and class status.[36]

The strength of racist images is manifested in the comments directed at women who are assumed to be good, upstanding white women. June, a businesswoman who is raising two biracial sons in suburban New Jersey, commented, "I think America still hates [white] women who sleep with black men. And when they see you with these children, they want to believe you adopted them, which is usually the first question people will ask: 'Did you adopt them?' I always just say, 'No, I slept with a black man.' "

June's comments highlight a few issues. First, she does not specify who constitutes "America." Whites may hate these women because they threaten the color line that maintains white privilege and power. At the same time, blacks may hate them because they threaten the unity of African Americans. Second, several white women talked to me about the frequency of the adoption question—one more attempt to explain their behavior. If women who appear to be good turn out to be polluted, white border patrollers become nervous. Their inability to tell "us" from "them" calls into question their own racial identity. The more the border patroller clings to an identity of racial superiority, the more he or she looks for ways to explain away these aberrant white women. Third, like June, many interracially married white women resist allowing whites to recategorize them in an attempt to regain or maintain a sense of superiority. "No, I used the good-old fashioned method" is a common retort to such questioners.

Not all white women resist border patrollers. Many succumb to the hostility and end their relationships with black men. Several white women told me they had temporarily ended their interracial relationship, each citing border patrolling as the reason. For instance, Barbara, the woman who gained forty pounds to avoid being seen as a prostitute, said:

> When I met my husband, he was the sweetest, kindest—
> he was a wonderful human being, everything I was
> looking for except for the color and at one point I was
> really apprehensive about it. The race thing really
> bothered me 'cause I didn't like being stared at and I
> didn't like people hating me. I didn't like how black
> women viewed me, and to white men I was a posses-
> sion. It's like, "you crossed the line." You know the
> feeling, like you have to be the lowest of the low to be
> with an African American. "Who are you trying to
> hurt?" It was just really sick. So I went away for a
> while.

Although she did eventually marry this "wonderful human being," she needed time away to think about race on a more sophisticated level—time to question her internalization of racist images and the color line.

The stereotype of black male sexuality converges with the myth of the chaste and virtuous good white woman, making white female–black male relationships the ones most patrolled by whites.[37] White men contend with a different type of border patrolling in a society that privileges both whiteness and maleness. Historically, white men who interracially marry were reported to come from lower economic classes and were at times designated as crazy.[38] Today the more common image that white interracially married men face is of being in the relationship solely for sex. These men may be seen as committing an individual transgression but are not held responsible for protecting whiteness. In her study of white supremacist publications, Abby Ferber found that "while relationships between white women and black men are condemned, and described as repulsive, relationships between white men and black women were common and remain beyond condemnation."[39] The lack of imagery about white male–black female relations reflects a history of silence among whites concerning their complicity in the rape of black women. Moreover, in a society in which whiteness (and maleness) represents power, privilege, and unearned advantage, many white men view their privilege in the world as normal. They risk "outing" these taken-for-granted privileges when they talk about race.[40]

The white men with whom I spoke were split about the importance of—even the existence of—border patrolling. Unlike black men, black women, and white women, they did not consistently talk about the effects of racialized images. When I asked, "As an interracially married white man, how do you think others view you?" responses were split: half the men spoke of border patrollers; the other half denied the importance of race in their lives and society. The first few times I heard white men deny or disregard the importance of racism and border patrolling, I was surprised. It took me some time and several more interviews to make sense of this.

Joe, the first interracially married white man I inter- viewed, lived in a predominantly white, upper-class com- munity about an hour from New York City. With his infant daughter on his lap and a tape recorder on the table, he began to unfold the details of his life. I asked how he thinks others view him. He responded, "I can't worry about what other people think. For a long time my wife worried, but once she got over that, we had a big wedding. . . . It took a lot to convince her that's how we should think about it, and I think she's more comfortable with that." He said that they do not have problems as an interracial couple, that everything is smooth. We were chatting after the interview when his wife walked into the room. She began to cite several problems they had faced because of their interracial relationship. When she referred to each incident, he nodded in agreement.

Several months later I interviewed Raymond, a white interracially married man living on Chicago's north side. Drinking coffee in a local café, he discussed the meaning of race in his life. When I asked him about how others view him, he replied staunchly, "I don't know, and I don't care. I never thought about it. I don't think about it. What do they think when they see my wife and me together? Pardon my language, but I don't give a shit what they think; I just don't give a shit. I go for months, and that never occupies my mind."

These men may be proving masculinity through a show of strength, rugged individualism, and disinterest and thus verbally disregard border patrolling and racial images. Each, however, repeatedly claimed that race does not matter. Instead, they believed the focus "should be on ethnic backgrounds" or on the fact that "we are all Americans." Men who did not want to recognize racial images tended not to recognize the privilege associated with whiteness, drawing instead on notions of meritocracy. Whether or not they recognized differences, they did not recognize power. Nevertheless, they used their power as white males to create a racial discussion with which they felt comfortable. For instance, Joe's comfort came from not having to hear any racially derogatory comments: "If somebody would make a derogatory comment, I would just say, 'My wife is black.' Usually I wouldn't even have to say, 'I don't want to hear comments like that'—they would just stop." Whiteness is about privilege and power. It is a privilege to be able to set the parameters of racial discussions and expect that others will comply. Moreover, the power of these professional white men overrides the power that white border patrollers may have to influence them.

In addition to proving masculinity, these men may be attempting to downplay the prevalent stereotype that interracial couples are together for sexual reasons only. For instance, Raymond repeatedly stated that his relationship was not about "jungle fever," a phrase that filmmaker Spike Lee popularized to suggest that interracial couples are attracted only because of sexual curiosity. At the end of our interview I asked Raymond if there was anything else he wanted to say. He answered, "Let people know that this is not about jungle fever. Race does not matter. I love my wife." His repeated references to jungle fever reflected his awareness of border patrolling despite his claim of color-blindness. Rather than critically thinking about race and the origins of such stereotypes, he defensively dismisses the significance of race.

Some white men did recognize and address the importance of racial images, border patrollers, and the relationship between race and power. The common thread for these men was that they had friendships and networks with black males before meeting their spouse. Through these male friends they began to recognize the privileges that remain invisible to so many other white men. The importance of friendships with black males cannot be understated. White men sit in a position of power because of both their race and sex. When sex differences are removed as a factor in their relationships, they can understand more clearly the ways in which race mediates power relations. This is not as obvious to white men who are introduced to blackness (and thus whiteness) through intimate relations with a woman.

Clancy, a fifty-year-old white man who grew up outside Chicago, had black roommates and friends in college. By time he met his wife he understood from his buddies the effects of racism in society. He spoke in detail about the border patrolling he faced from the white teachers at the Chicago elementary school where he taught after getting married: "My wife and I walked into a meeting with the white teachers and the people from the neighborhood, and it sent those people into conniptions. I won't forget that. It was my first year teaching there, and from then on it was like, 'God have mercy on my soul,' I was a dead person in that school and that stayed with me for seventeen years—the whole time I was there." In this case, Clancy's teaching position was continually threatened by white border patrollers.

Peter, a white minister living on Chicago's South Side, had graduated from a black seminary in the southern United States. As the only white in many situations, he was immersed in black culture. The privileges and power bestowed to whites in a system of whiteness and the richness of black culture became visible to him. Like Clancy, he recognized and addressed the border patrolling he encountered from whites. In the following case, Peter had just been named the pastor of a white church in a white working-class neighborhood in Cleveland: "I had gotten moved to a white church. That turned out to be two years from hell. The church did not want me to be appointed there. They actually had a special meeting after they got wind of who was coming; 95 percent of the church did not want me there because I was interracially married. The first church meeting I was at, the chair asked for further motions. One person said, 'I make a motion that the reverend resign from this church.' " Peter laughed about the absurdity of the situation and then continued: "The first sermon, attendance was over one hundred; everyone came out to see the show. From then on, attendance never got above sixty, so basically about forty people boycotted the whole time I was there. I had people who still attended but resigned all their offices." In addition, church members began a letter-writing campaign to the bishop accusing Peter of various wrongdoings—for example, claiming he had taken all the Bibles out of the church. Peter and his family eventually moved to a black church in Chicago. The Ohio church members who had resigned their offices returned to them after he left.

Privileges granted to people with white skin have been institutionalized and made largely invisible to the beneficiaries. With overwhelming power in society, why do individual whites insist on border patrolling? As economic insecurity heightens and demographics show that whites are losing numerical majority status, the desire to scapegoat people of color, especially the poor, also heightens. As whites lose their economic footing, they claim white skin as a liability. Far from recognizing whiteness as privilege, they become conscious of whiteness only when defining themselves as innocent victims of "unjust" laws, including affirmative action.[41] In their insecurity they cling to images that promote feelings of superiority. This, of course, requires a racial hierarchy and a firm essentialist color line. Border patrolling helps to maintain the myth of purity and thus a color line created to ensure that whites maintain privileges and power.

Black Border Patrolling. Some blacks in interracial relationships discover, for the first time, a lack of acceptance from black communities. Others experienced border patrolling before their marriage, perhaps because of hobbies and interests, class, politics, educational goals, skin tone, vernacular, or friendship networks. Patrolling takes on new proportions, however, when they go the "other way" and marry a white person. While all relationships with individuals not seen as black are looked down on, relationships with whites represent the gravest transgression. Interracially married black women and men often believe they are viewed as having lost their identity and culture—that they risk being seen as "no longer really black." Before their interracial marriage, most called black communities their home, the place from which they gained a sense of humanity, where they gained cultural and personal affirmation. During their interracial relationship many discovered black border patrolling. Cathy Cohen suggests that "those failing to meet indigenous standards of blackness find their life chances threatened not only by dominant institutions or groups, but also by their lack of access to indigenous resources and support."[42] Interracially involved blacks needed to carefully weigh their decision to cross the color line.

George, a black man, lives with his wife, Dorothy, a white woman, and their two young children in Montclair, New Jersey, a racially mixed suburb of New York City. I drove along the town's big, clean, tree-lined streets one Sunday morning to meet with George in his home. During our interview he explained that he had dated a white girl in high school and was aware of how blacks and whites respond to such a relationship. Nonetheless, a recent event at his Manhattan workplace troubled him. Bill, a black male co-worker, told him:

"I couldn't marry a white woman. How about you?"

I said, "I am married to a white woman."

"You joking me, George! Big strong handsome brother like you!"

I said, "Yo, man, I don't know what all that handsome stuff you comin' with."

He said, "All jokes aside, George, you telling me you went the other way?"

I said, "There's nothing wrong with that."

And he's like "Oh, George, I don't believe it."

He was just solemn after that and looked down, so I said, "Bill, does that mean we're not going to be friends anymore?"

He goes, "No, man, you still my man."

He gave me the ole handshake; I said, "Bill, no, man, you frontin' now."

He said, "I'm just surprised, you know. You never told me about your wife."

The implication here is that a "strong brother" would not sell out his community like this; only weak men would do that. Before this confrontation George had been an integral part of many conversations at work about race, racism, and black culture. After it he found "they'll be talking about something totally in the black culture. I come into the room and be listening; and when I would put my opinion in, the conversation would end—just like that. The room goes empty. . . . because I'm married to a white woman, blacks figure my culture is gone; it's shot." He is accused of having lost connectedness to African Americans, being weak, and marrying a white woman to escape his blackness.

Blacks in interracial relationships defend themselves against accusations of weakness, neurosis, and betrayal. In *Black Skin, White Masks*, Frantz Fanon writes about black men in interracial relationships: "I marry white culture, white beauty, white whiteness. When my restless hands caress those white breasts, they grasp white civilization and dignity and make them mine."[43] In his psychoanalytic interpretation of the effects of colonization and racism, Fanon suggests that many black men who intermarry suffer from neurosis created in a world in which black men are not valued and thus do not value themselves. They think that a relationship with a white woman will validate them—that is, whiten them. Of black women, Fanon writes, "It is because the Negress feels inferior that she aspires to win admittance into the white world."[44] Without acknowledging the pain caused by border patrolling and the desire many interracially married blacks have to maintain strong ties with other blacks, Fanon labels black men and black women in interracial relationships as pathological and neurotic.

More recently, Paul Rosenblatt and his colleagues conducted a study of forty-two multiracial couples in the Minneapolis–St. Paul area. They conclude that many African Americans feel that "it is inappropriate to choose as a partner somebody from the group that has been oppressing African Americans."[45] Many black border patrollers have an overriding concern about loyalty to the race. If an individual is not being loyal, then he or she is explained away as weak, acting in ways that are complicit with the oppression of other black Americans. In "Essentialism and the Complexities of Racial Identity," Michael Eric Dyson suggests, "Loyalty to race has been historically construed as primary and unquestioning allegiance to the racial quest for freedom and the refusal to betray that quest to personal benefit or the diverting pursuit of lesser goals. Those who detour from the prescribed path are labeled 'sellouts,' 'weak,' 'traitors,' or 'Uncle Toms.' "[46] Thus, black men and women face differing social realities and forms of patrolling.

An overwhelming percentage of black-white couples involve a black male and a white female at a time when there are "more single women in the black community than single men."[47] Many black men are hindered by a racist educational system and job market that make them less desirable for marriage. Many others are scooped into the prison industrial complex. High-profile athletes and entertainers who marry white women confirm for many that black men who are educated and earn a good living sell out, attempting to buy white status through their interracial relationship.[48] Beyond issues of money and status, many black women see black male–white female interracial relationships "as a rejection of black women's beauty, [and] as a failure to acknowledge and reward the support that black women give black men."[49] In *Rooted against the Wind*, Gloria Wade-Gayles writes about the pain and feeling of rejection that black women experience when they see black men with white women:

> We see them, and we feel abandoned. We feel abandoned because we have been abandoned in so many ways, by so many people, and for so many centuries. We are the group of women furthest removed from the concept of beauty and femininity which invades almost every spot of the planet, and as a result, we are taught not to like ourselves, or, as my student said, not to believe that we can ever do enough or be enough to be loved or desired.[50]

Black women and men may both feel a sense of rejection when they see an interracial couple, but for each that sense of rejection comes from a different place. In a society in which women's worth is judged largely by beauty—more specifically, Eurocentric standards of beauty—black women are presumed to be the farthest removed from such a standard. Men's worth is judged largely by their educational and occupational status, two primary areas in which black men are undermined in a racist system. Black men with few educational and job opportunities lack status in the marriage market. Thus, when black men see a black woman with a white man, they may be reminded of the numerous ways in which the white-supremacist system has denied them opportunities. The privilege and power granted to whites, particularly to white males, is paraded in front of them; and they see the black women in these relationships as complicit with the oppressor.

I met Parsia, a successful businesswoman and a black interracially married mother living in Connecticut, through a family friend. Having grown up in a close-knit African American community, she was uncertain if she wanted to marry interracially and risk losing the support of that community. Now happily married and the mother of a beautiful little girl, she is still very aware of border patrolling. For this reason she prefers not to bring her husband to some areas in Harlem and to black-centered events:

> African Americans do view blacks in interracial relationships as turncoats. There is a pervasive belief in the African American community that it is much more difficult to maintain your identity in an interracial relationship. I believe that once blacks see me as part of an interracial couple, it changes their perception of me right away. They disrespect me as another black person, and then they just disregard my belonging to the community, and suddenly I become the outsider—an outsider because I am with him.

Her fears are not unfounded. One day she and her husband were walking in Philadelphia when a young black man accosted them:

> If I had been alone and this young brother was hassling me in any way, I would have stopped, turned around, and said, "Look, why are you bothering me? What's the deal here?" But I didn't feel at all that I could have this conversation with this young man. He was so hostile, and the source of his hostility was totally his perception of black-white relationships, and there was nothing I could say to change that perception.

This young border patroller may be responding to a belief that Parsia is a race traitor. She is no longer an insider worthy of respect but an outsider who signifies neurosis in the form of self-hate and community betrayal—perhaps the highest form of betrayal. The prospect of rejection by other African Americans is enough for many blacks to deny, hide, or avoid interracial relationships. Border patrolling from other blacks, racism from whites, and the prospect of struggling alone in a racist society seem too high a price; so many who enter interracial relationships end them in short time.

Today there are no longer legal sanctions against interracial marriage, but de facto sanctions remain. At times, family and friends exert pressure to end the interracial relationship; at other times, pressure may come from the border patrolling of strangers. Even if the relationship is clandestine, thoughts of how friends, family members, co-workers, employers, and the general public might respond can deter people from moving forward in a relationship. In each of the following cases the couples did get back together eventually, but all the black woman took some time away from the relationship to make this choice.

Lisa met her white husband when she was a college student at a historically black college in the South.

> [I was] the only female in the jazz orchestra, [so] there were all these [black] guys saying, "Why are you with this white guy?" And one band member would make racial comments about "Don't marry whitey, don't trust whitey, don't do this for whitey." This guy in the band tried to talk me out of marrying Peter. I had some apprehension, so I broke up with him and told him I did not want to develop a relationship.

Parsia explains why she temporarily ended her relationship before finally deciding to marry her white husband, Joe:

> When I met Joe, I was really resistant to dating across racial lines. No way would I do that. It took me a very long time to get over that and deal with those feelings, biases, and expectations. I expected friends would feel very uncomfortable socializing with us. I still do believe that there is a certain language that blacks have when we are apart from other races, when we are alone socially. That's a very important part of my life, and I expected that I might lose that, and that was a very fearful thing for me. The more I felt him getting closer, the more I started seeing the possibility of longevity in the relationship, the more afraid I got. I was terrified that I would be in an interracial relationship for the rest of my life, so I pulled back in a big way and we broke up. There was definitely a shame and a guilt I had to get over because I felt that by dating interracially I was betraying black men.

Her fear reflects her reliance on other African Americans for mutual support in a white-supremacist system. Moreover, her observation that "there is a certain language that blacks have when we are apart from other races" indicates a shared cultural identity that creates and demands the enforcement of borders.

In some cases parents and family reinforce reservations about crossing over. Quisha, like Parsia, broke up with her white boyfriend, Raymond, because she needed time to think about what life would be like in an interracial relationship. "I was really excited about him and told my mom, and she just had a heart attack because he was white. I totally did not expect this from her. She would call every-day and was just hammering it into me to just forget this—and so I really badly and abruptly broke it off with Raymond. He was a real gentleman; he kept calling to find out what happened, and I totally blew him off." She explained her underlying fears as she discussed how she handles people staring at her: "I can feel my grandmother and my mother and my aunts disapproving in those stares, so that's intimidating." Lisa, Parsia, and Quisha all married the men they had left, but they needed time to think about risks, their own understandings of race and community, and what it means to be a black woman in the United States.

They are three of the many black women in interracial relationships who challenge the idea that white men are responsible for the low number of black female–white male interracial marriages. Theorists attempting to explain motives behind interracial marriages have often pointed to the low number of these marriages as evidence that white men are choosing not to marry black women.[51] These theorists suggest that white men are least likely to intermarry with black women because they would gain nothing in these marriages: no money, no status. My research, however, demonstrates the power of black women. The stories they share directly challenge longheld motive myths that imply that black women would marry white men if only white men would choose them. On the contrary, in each of the relationships just discussed, the black woman instigated a breakup. Perhaps their understanding of what it means to be strong, dedicated, and connected to black communities is responsible for the lower numbers of black female–white male marriages.

Border patrolling plays a central role in life decisions and the reproduction of the color line. As decisions are made to enter and remain in an interracial relationship, the color line is challenged and racial identities shift. Many blacks spoke of the growth they experienced because of their interracial relationship and border patrolling. Parsia explains, "I used to be real concerned about how I would be perceived and that as an interracially married female I would be taken less seriously in terms of my dedication to African American causes. I'm not nearly as concerned anymore. I would hold my record up to most of those in single-race relationships, and I would say, 'Okay, let's go toe to toe, and you tell me who's making the biggest difference,' and so I don't worry about it anymore." Identities, once grounded in the presumed acceptance of other black Americans, have become more reflective. Acceptance can no longer be assumed. Definitions of what it means to be black are reworked. Likewise, because of border patrolling, many whites in interracial relationships began to acknowledge that race matters. Whiteness becomes visible in their claims to racial identity.

### Rebound Racism

When whites enter an interracial relationship they experience racism, albeit indirectly. In these cases racism is directed at the black partner but also affects the white partner. Talking specifically about white women, Ruth Frankenberg defines such *rebound racism* as "a force that owes its existence and direction to an earlier aim and impact, yet retains enough force to wound. . . . While it is hard to measure pain, it is safe to say both that the racism that rebounds on white women has spent some of its force in the original impact it made on their nonwhite partners and that white women nonetheless feel its impact."[52] The effect can be financial, emotional, or physical. While the white partner is not the intended victim, she or he is in a relationship with someone who is. For example, if the black partner does not get a fair raise, this affects the financial well-being of the white partner. If the black partner is given unfair traffic tickets or treated badly at work, this spills over into the family. The white partner with emotional, financial, and familial ties to the black partner gains a sense of the pain and disadvantage doled out to people of color in a system of whiteness.

Candace, like the other interracially married whites with whom I spoke, found that when she is alone, away from her family, whites treat her "perfectly all right." When she is with her family, however, "it's a whole different thing." The *whole different thing* is border patrolling and rebound racism and includes hostile stares and rude treatment in stores and restaurants. June discovered rebound racism while trying to catch a cab with her husband:

> The worst thing is getting a cab in New York City; that is the worst feeling I have ever had with my husband. It was having to get a cab on my own; and then when he would come up, they would drive away. Oh, that to me is the worst because then I could almost feel his pain and feel how awful it must be to deal with this in every aspect of your life, every day. It was so humiliating and so demeaning. I hate those cab drivers. They would pull up; and as soon as he came up, they would drive right away. I mean just leave you standing there with your hand stretched out.

June's pain was directly related to what was happening to her black partner. Because of this and other experiences of rebound racism, she can no longer take race for granted. It now becomes associated with humiliation and hatefulness; a color-blind perspective is no longer possible or desirable. For June the color line is not a distant separation of whites and blacks but a means for protecting white supremacy.

Several years ago my husband and I were driving from

Chicago to visit his family. We knew that New Jersey's highway patrol had a reputation for hassling African Americans. We also knew that we would not get to New Jersey until about midnight. We stopped for gas at a busy highway station before we crossed the state line. It is important to go to roadside gas stations because you don't want to get off the main highway when traveling alone together as an interracial couple—especially at night. It was Philip's turn to drive. Much to my chagrin, he was maintaining a steady fifty-five miles per hour. I was unsuccessfully nudging him to speed it up so we could get to his parents' at a reasonable hour when the flashing lights appeared from behind. A young white male police officer pulled us over. Without giving a reason, even when we asked, he demanded our registration, proof of insurance, and both of our licenses. He then put my husband in his car and told me to stay put. After what seemed like an eternity, the officer came to my window and asked me a series of questions: "How long have you two known each other? What is your line of work? What does he do? How long has he been in law school? Where are you going? What are his parents' names? What are your sisters' names? How long have you been in graduate school? What are you studying?" I wanted to say, "Racist cops," but I did my best to answer his questions politely, all the time mindful that he still had Philip in his cruiser. Apparently our answers satisfied the cop because he let Philip return to the car and, without explanation, handed us our licenses and registration, telling us to have a nice night. I don't know how, in the dark of night, he could have seen us in the car. Perhaps he intended to harass a black man and, when he found me there, thought he had hit a jackpot—you know, the old "this must be a kidnapping" or "this white woman must be a prostitute." Perhaps he was able to see us and thought he had found himself a real live interracial Bonnie and Clyde cruising along the Jersey interstate in a Hyundai Excel.

In this instance I experienced rebound racism. I doubt I would have been pulled over if I were by myself or with another white person. While I was not driving that time, I have been on other occasions. I was pulled over once with Philip in the car and given a ticket. I was pulled over several times while alone, and each time received a warning and was let off without ticket. Here, not receiving tickets is a factor of white privilege; receiving a ticket with my husband is a factor of rebound racism and possibly border patrolling.

For many whites, rebound racism makes them more aware of white privilege. Candace told me:

> I have grown tremendously through this relationship. I understand the privilege of skin color. I might have known what that concept was if I would have read it in a book but not the reality of understanding that in life. If I was in an all-white marriage, I think I would have taken an awful lot for granted, and I wouldn't be as sensitive to many things. I often think, "How could I have missed that before?" and because it's suddenly placed in front of you, you're more sensitive.

Many interracially married whites no longer feel they are connected to or benefit from a larger system of whiteness. In *The Color of Water: A Black Man's Tribute to His White Mother*, James McBride writes of his mother's refusal to "acknowledge her whiteness," instead claiming that she was light-skinned. McBride "initially accepted [this claim] as fact but at some point later decided it was not true."[53] Without the opportunity to hear from his mother, we can only speculate why she claimed to be black, when, as her son documents, so many others saw her as a white woman. Maybe she did not want her children to live with the discomfort of being mixed in a single-race world. If she claimed to be black (and could convince others), then her children would be black without question. As a low-income mother of twelve black children, she may have identified most closely with political and social issues important to many African Americans. Perhaps she saw blackness as a privilege. Identities are, after all, shaped by our daily experiences. Maria P. P. Root writes that "the love a child receives, and the faces that reflect who they are, are likely to be some shade of brown. The children will likely internalize an identification with those from whom they come."[54] Isn't it possible that adults may do the same?[55]

Some interracially married whites begin to essentialize all other whites as bad and racist and all blacks as good and victims. By essentializing whites as inherently and universally racist, these interracially married whites have created an internal conflict. If all whites are racist, then *all* must include themselves. Attempts to describe their own identities as antiracist become convoluted. For instance, June said, "I've become much more black, which is a very troublesome thing because people don't know it when they see me." She laughed. "I'm always making excuses for myself, but that's where I see myself. I am pretty anti-white, and I know I look stupid in groups talking about 'those white people,' but I do and I just hope that they'll think I'm just very light-skinned." The lack of available language to describe racial identities outside of the black-white dichotomy coupled with the essentialist thinking that all whites are bad leaves some interracially married whites with no option other than claiming a black identity. This is one way in which individuals contend with and get caught in essentialist language and thought. Rather than understanding rebound racism as one more strategy used to keep the color line intact, they reinforce the color line by calling themselves exceptions to the rule.

Barbara spoke of making T-shirts for herself and other

antiracist, interracially involved whites. The logo on the shirt would read, "One of the good ones," a saying a black friend used when vouching for her to other blacks. The assumption underlying her logo is that a few individuals can be exceptions but the color line remains stable, fixed, and essential. Others have begun to think about their racial identities outside of an essentialist paradigm. This is a difficult task given the lack of anti-essentialist language. In "Representations of Whiteness in the Black Imagination," bell hooks recalls a conversation she had with an interracially involved black woman: "We talk about the way white people who shift locations, as her companion has done, begin to see the world differently. Understanding how racism works, he can see the way in which whiteness acts to terrorize without seeing himself as bad, or all white people as bad, and all black people as good."[56]

### Intensified Racism

While the white partner experiences rebound racism, the black partner often faces escalated forms of racism because of the interracial relationship. In this case, racism normally directed at blacks is intensified because they have dared to cross the color line through marriage or partnership. Such was the case of the black man killed in suburban Baltimore because he walked with his white girlfriend in a white neighborhood. Black males most often spoke of intensified racism. This is nothing new. During Reconstruction white southerners were manic in their attempts to stop miscegenation and protect white womanhood. Racial hygienic platforms were central to this goal. The system of whiteness was formed in large part through the rape and exploitation of black women and the simultaneous lynching of black men for supposed crimes against white women. Julien, a black interracially married father of five living in a western suburb of Chicago, spoke of the intensified racism he experienced. During our first interview he mentioned that his children had been to his workplace but that his wife never had. The children look very much like their mother except they have caramel-colored skin and curly hair. Given Julien's brown skin and hair texture, most blacks would suspect that his children are multiracial. Many whites, however, are not raised to think about skin color using terms such as *honey, cinnamon, brown,* or *caramel.* They are not part of the language that whites incorporate into their racial thinking. An individual is either white or black. Thus, Julien felt safe bringing his children to his workplace but not his wife. I asked him to explain why. "I have no way to prove this" he said, " but if they were to find out I was interracially married, I would have been fired because there were some incidents where black guys were going out with white girls and actually brought them to work. I just learned from that experience not to bring her; they got fired. The black guys who were dealing with white girls; they trumped up charges and fired them. She's never been to my work, and she never will." At work, he allows his white bosses to assume his wife is black. Julien is describing a racist system in which, for blacks, crossing the color line can be life-threatening either directly or through denial of the means necessary to survive.

## Conclusion

Unlike transracially adopted and multiracial people who are raised across the color line, people in interracial relationships discover borderism when they decide to cross the line. This unique form of discrimination, grounded in a racist and segregated society, is always at work even when multiracial family members are not present. Yet by examining the experiences of multiracial family members, we can

see the myriad ways in which the color line is both reproduced and resisted. Because interracially married people are
often raised in single-race worlds, they have internalized borderism. Thus, part of the decision to become involved interracially includes the need to overcome internalized borderist
thoughts. Most of them begin questioning color-blind and
essentialist perspectives and learn to understand race as
more fluid and complex. Skin color and physical features
become just one set of criteria used to think about community and belonging. Many of the people I interviewed
referred to this growth process (although not all interracially married people accept the invitation to rethink race).

In a society that often rejects people who cross the color
line, individuals involved in such relationships have much
to consider before making a permanent commitment. Given
the significance of race in our society, a basic choice that all
couples contend with is whether or not to stay together in
the face of borderism. A few individuals claimed that there
was no decision; they fell in love, and that was it. For most
others, however, a life across the color line and facing borderism did not look all that inviting and in fact was enough
to cause some to terminate their relationships.[57] While the
number of people involved in interracial relationships are not
known, we do know that in 1995 the census bureau estimated
that there were only 246,000 black-white interracial marriages
in the United States.[58] This is quite a small percentage considering that in the same year there were more than 50 mil-
lion total marriages.[59] Borderism and its various components
are strong and painful enough to keep black-white interracial marriages the least common marriage pattern for both
blacks and whites.

# 2

## Redlines

## and Color

## Lines

"Love thy neighbor" and "stick with your own" could be read as contradictory statements. Sticking with our own implies a distrust in, disdain for, or disinterest in those not defined as members of the in group. Yet in the United States these messages fit well together. In racially segregated cities and neighborhoods, loving our neighbor implies sticking with our own. According to Douglas Massey and Nancy Denton, the housing market is hyper-segregated.[1] Fair housing advocates warn that, as the nation becomes more diverse (and less white), we risk becoming balkanized rather than being a country with cooperating groups that share resources.[2] The housing market has been a primary means for maintaining the color line in the United States. Through the institutionalized and discriminatory practices in the housing industry, the color line has been clarified and strengthened. Discriminatory practices have not only given whites an advantage but have allowed many people, particularly those in racially segregated suburbs, to deny that race matters. Pervasive discrimination coupled with contemporary amnesia about the centrality of race strengthens the color line. The strength of that line is then reflected in the treatment multiracial families receive when they attempt to fit their racially mixed households into a racially segregated housing market. In particular, the childhood experiences of multiracial and transracially adopted people highlight the role that housing plays in other aspects of life such as issues of identity, social status, and friendship networks.

This chapter demonstrates that the color line has been created and maintained in the housing market through unfair and racist practices. Underlying such practices is a racist belief that whites are inherently valuable and thus deserving of good housing, loans, and other subsidies, while blacks are devalued and denied access to good housing and loans. The outcome has been the segregated and unequal housing market—the dual-housing market. The experiences of multiracial family members in this market show how the color line is patrolled on both the individual and institutional levels. The strategies they employ to negotiate borderism highlight the social construction of the color line while uncovering the myth of the essentialist color line.

### Redlining and the Color Line: A Brief History

Redlining, the process of denying mortgage, loans, and insurance to particular neighborhoods, has been a primary means of creating and maintaining the color line. Basing their actions on racist and classist assumptions, whites have redlined entire black neighborhoods. As chief of housing and civil enforcement at the U.S. Department of Justice, Paul Hancock acknowledged the wealth of evidence proving the existence of such practices: "Mortgage lenders act as expediters for whites and gatekeepers for blacks."[3] Without mortgages, loans, and insurance, homes and businesses cannot be bought, sold, or repaired. Existing homes and businesses that are denied loans and insurance collapse one after another.[4] Those who own property see it being devalued and underappraised. Schools, heavily dependent on local property taxes, begin to deteriorate along with other local institutions. Without the opportunity for a good education, children are unable to obtain the credentials necessary to compete in the job market. Thus, they will not be able to afford to live in an area where their children will have access to better education. Manning Marable stresses that "all-black or all-Latino neighborhoods in themselves aren't the problem; the destruction of jobs, substandard housing, inadequate public healthcare, deteriorating schools and public transportation systems in those neighborhoods are."[5] Unfair housing practices have been a central means of denying entire groups of people, particularly blacks and Latinos, an equal opportunity to make it—a way of reinforcing a color line that is then explained as natural and static.

Northern cities are notorious for high levels of segregation.[6] New York City and Chicago, the two areas where I concentrated my research, share a history of engaging in discriminatory housing practices. New York City has created itself through slum clearance and redevelopment, producing in the process a large displaced population of mainly blacks and Latinos. In Chicago, blacks were historically restricted to the overcrowded and inferior housing in the "black belt" on the South Side. As blacks began demanding more affordable and better housing, whites violently defended their neighborhoods and then began the flight to the segregated and federally subsidized suburbs. While segregation dropped slightly in Chicago between 1970 and 1990, New York City's level of segregation rose.[7] Many historical and social differences exist between the two cities, yet they are quite similar in their current level of housing segregation. The dual-housing market is precisely the place to watch multiracial family members search for safe, affordable, and comfortable neighborhoods.

In 1965 Karl and Alma Taeuber argued that the invasion-succession model (which claims that as blacks move in whites flee, leaving a segregated neighborhood) was common in U.S. cities.[8] In *American Apartheid*, Douglas Massey and Nancy Denton point out that a process called racial tipping starts when the first white family in the neighborhood moves out. As that family moves out, a black family moves in. This pattern continues until the invasion-succession model appears to be in effect.[9] Peter Wood and Barrett Lee argue that neighborhoods change largely because of a self-fulfilling prophecy: if whites believe that neighborhood change is a matter of fact, they will sell their homes and make it a fact.[10] Blatant forms of panic peddling have been outlawed, yet many whites cling to racist images that create an inevitable succession model: beliefs that housing prices will drop, crime rates rise, and school standards decline. Whites pull out, mortgage lenders begin to redline, and together they make the invasion-succession model a reality.[11] Basing their arguments on what has been called an inevitable process, many people call mixed-race neighborhoods simply transitional neighborhoods. Some mixed-race neighborhoods are indeed only mixed during the transition phase and are thus hostile areas on the way to becoming resegregated.

In 1968, a year after the Loving decision that struck down antimiscegenation laws, the Fair Housing Act was passed. The act declared that discrimination in the housing market was illegal and that blacks could, by law, buy homes in areas maintained as white only. Previously, landlords, realtors, insurers, and lenders used overt, often government-approved and encouraged, discriminatory practices. For example, until 1950 the National Association of Realtors advised against bringing in "members of any race or nationality, or any individual whose presence will clearly be detrimental to property values in the neighborhood."[12] The 1938 Federal Housing Administration (FHA)'s *Underwriting Manual* noted, "If a neighborhood is to retain stability, it is necessary that properties shall continue to be occupied by the same social and racial classes. A change in social or racial occupancy generally contributes to instability and a decline in values."[13] The issue, then, was not about sameness, as the FHA initially suggested; rather, it was about the belief that blacks and whites are essentially different and that whites are inherently superior and more valuable. The housing market reflects a color line that institutional representatives (realtors, lenders, brokers, and insurers) have constructed and maintained through laws, manuals, and actions. Based on essentialist and racist beliefs about the inherent value of human beings, the color line, stark and bold, makes housing a detriment to the economic well-being of most blacks, is a source of wealth for many whites, and the basis of great social and economic difficulty for multiracial families. Even after the passing of the Fair Housing Act, discriminatory practices continued, albeit more covertly.[14] The irony is that if the color line were based on essential race differences, whites wouldn't have to work so hard to maintain it.

Blacks have a strong history of protesting the mass inequality in the housing market. Freedom marches, riots, and other forms of protest remind others that the FHA's quest for sameness was really about strengthening a color line that continued to protect white privilege. Until the civil rights and black power movements, institutional practices protected white neighborhoods. Only after the movements took hold were white areas forced open. As institutional mechanisms began failing to protect the color line for the white working class, individual whites engaged in overt forms of racism. The color line was threatened because, as these whites saw it, their private property, the cornerstone of a capitalist system and their own futures, was going to be devalued. Without a claim to a valuable piece of property, their status was threatened.

Historically, white working-class neighborhoods have responded with greater hostility than other groups have to blacks moving into "their" community.[15] When blacks began demanding access to better housing, they were not eyeing property in Chicago's Gold Coast or the Upper West Side of Manhattan. They began pushing for affordable housing in affordable neighborhoods—working-class, white neighborhoods. Panic peddling worked in these areas because whites believed the basic racist tenet used by realtors: whites are more valuable than blacks; thus, anything owned by blacks will be devalued. Moreover, working-class communities may have been overtly hostile because they often lack the political and economic clout to ensure their home values.[16] As history reflects, members of the white working class often patrol the color line from their front yards. Without savings and investments, many see their homes as their primary source of economic security in case of hard times. Any threat to the value of their property is met with hostility. Rather than struggle for better economic safety nets for all, they have historically scapegoated blacks as the cause of the devaluation.

Whites who live in wealthier communities, such as the Gold Coast or the Upper West Side, can afford, at least on the surface, to accept a few blacks in the area. The housing market places economic constraints on who can afford to live in such a community. Wealthier white communities are generally built in desirable geographic locations and have the amenities people desire, such as good schools, museums, shops, and access to transportation and parks. Only people willing and able to pay for such amenities can live in these areas. Given the mass inequities in the educational system and job market, smaller percentages of blacks can afford such communities (and many choose not to live in them even when resources are not the issue). Individuals in wealthier areas tend to have access to institutional clout and perhaps political clout. They can exercise their racist and classist will through institutional and political means and avoid stone throwing and cross burning. As such, residents can claim not to be racist. Wealthier white communities can forgo overt individual racist actions because they have the protection of institutional racism and classism.

Throughout the 1960s and into the 1970s, white working-class neighborhoods were turned inside out and upside down. Buying into realtors' panic peddling, residents were fleeing to federally subsidized suburbs. Blacks were trying to keep their heads above water while fighting for freedom. Multiracial families were caught in the crosscurrents of hostility. Within two or three years a neighborhood might change from all white to all black. Communities would appear racially diverse; multiracial and black families would move in only to discover hostile white neighbors fleeing. The neighborhood was in transition.

Andrea, a forty-three-year-old mixed-race woman with racially ambiguous features, recalls:

> We always tried to live in racially mixed neighbor-
> hoods, but usually what happened was that as soon as
> blacks moved in, the whites moved. When we moved
> in, we were like the second black family to move here.
> . . . everybody's house went up for sale. A lot of it is the
> real estate agents' fault because they would perpetuate

this thing by threatening that property values will go down and of course it happened because they made it happen. "The niggers are moving into your neighborhood; you better sell quick!"

When Andrea first began high school, there were "a few blacks in the school, and it took like four to five years before all the whites were gone."

This history has repeated itself over and over again in urban neighborhoods across the nation. After paying inflated prices for their homes, black and multiracial families soon discovered their property was being undervalued. For African Americans, the struggle against devaluation in the housing market was part of a larger struggle for social justice and meant battling the entire housing industry, including the federal government, banks, insurers, policymakers, and individual racist ambassadors of this industry (realtors, lenders, landlords, and racist white neighbors).

## Multiracial Families and the Dual-Housing Market

Multiracial families in the housing market face segregation imposed by white-controlled institutions and separation desired by many members of black communities. In black neighborhoods multiracial families face border patrolling, the intensity of which is tied to larger racial politics. For instance, during the peak of the black power movement, multiracial family members underwent intense patrolling. Today, many report feeling comfortable and accepted in black neighborhoods. The borderism they experience in white neighborhoods plays out primarily on the institutional level, with one major exception: the classroom and the playground. In racially mixed neighborhoods, multiracial family members find places in which they do not have to contend with intense, daily border patrolling. Even in these areas, however, the color line is being actively reproduced.

### Multiracial Families in Black Neighborhoods: Border Patrolling and Color Line

Attempts to devalue African Americans and all but eliminate their ability to compete in U.S. society has been met with strong resistance. Black liberation struggles have not been about wanting to live among whites but about gaining equality and access to necessary resources. The demand for justice took on new dimensions during the 1960s and 1970s with the growth of nationalist movements.[17] Most blacks were searching for a connection with other African Americans, turning inward for affirmation and celebration while struggling for liberation. Detecting the line between insider and outsider became important. Calls for authenticity (behaviors that show that an individual can be a trusted insider who really understands what it is to be black) became prominent. Individuals who looked white, were white, or had immediate white family members were suspected. Those who could display the appropriate cultural capital were accepted as insiders.[18] (*Cultural capital,* as I am using the term, includes the behaviors, actions, thoughts, tastes, ancestry, and choices that are rewarded within respective communities at particular points in history.) The cultural capital that may bring rewards and status among African Americans is not necessarily going to bring rewards in the mainstream white society and vice versa. For people of color in a white-supremacist society, acceptance by other people of color is an important means of strength, happiness, and affirmation. But acceptance is neither granted nor denied based on skin color alone. Individuals are expected to display an understanding of and desire to be part of the community.

This may include expressing particular political perspectives; sharing social experiences; speaking, looking, and carrying oneself in certain ways; and perhaps denying relatives who are considered outsiders.[19] Those unable or unwilling to fulfill the criteria and display the appropriate cultural capital were jettisoned to the margins—denied insider status.

Many multiracial family members found themselves relegated to these margins. Such families often have a connection to whiteness—perhaps a white family member or lighter-skinned children and access to goods and services that blacks are often denied. They are suspected, not because they do not conform to community standards, although this may be true, but because they appear to be situated closer to white power and privilege. Thus, multiracial family members in black neighborhoods, particularly in the 1960s and 1970s, faced some hardships. Light-skinned people had to prove they belonged to the community. Light-skinned, mixed-race people with a white parent were even one more step removed and had a tougher task of proving they belonged. Cynthia Nakashima writes, "Multiracial people who are part white are seen as inherently 'whitewashed'; they are harassed for their light skin or light hair, their loyalty is always in question, and they are not allowed to discuss their multiraciality if they want to be included as legitimate 'persons of color.' "[20] There is no way to prove one is authentically white outside of appearance backed by a white family tree. Because blacks do not call upon the myth of purity they can (and do) open their borders to include a broader group of people who prove their blackness and meet some version of the one-drop rule. This history has prompted Lisa Jones to observe that "black folks have welcomed differences in their communities more than most Americans."[21] Yet the need to prove by displaying the appropriate cultural capital can get burdensome.

Several people I interviewed lived in black neighborhoods during the civil rights and black power movements, some of which had gone through a transition from white to black. These people talked about being chastised for not trying hard enough to be black. Andrea's refusal to deny her mixed heritage was exacerbated by her ambiguous appearance: "I was at a party one of the high school clubs gave, and this was a year the Blackstone Rangers were getting big. This one guy came over and said something to me about being white. And I said, 'I'm not white. My father's black and my mother's white. You don't know anything about me, so don't talk to me.' Next thing I know, some friends are whisking me off to this room telling me to stay there because there was going to be some trouble. Next thing, the party was over. It was scary because they were looking to beat me up." Unable to change her physical appearance and her parents, Andrea and other multiracial and transracially adopted people had to find different ways to prove they were black enough.

"What it boils down to is that this was the sixties, the era of 'say it loud; I'm black, and I'm proud,' " recalled Lauren, a transracially adopted woman with racially ambiguous features. "And it was not enough to be black; you had to prove it, always. And if you were a light-skinned black, then you had to prove it more than anyone else." For Lauren and others this sometimes meant denying white parents, spending a lot of time in the sun, using the hippest language possible, and voicing militant politics. Of course, blackness is much more complex than a tan and hip language, but in a child's mind these were what mattered. Sometimes the denial of the white parent was central to the child's ability to feel comfortable and accepted. Lauren was already very light skinned with light-brown hair and green eyes, and unfortunately she attended the same school in which her white adoptive father was a social worker: "I had to deal with other people's attitudes: 'Well, I thought you said that you were mixed. I thought you said you were black. I saw your father.' Also, my dad and I used to take the El to school. Our stop was at 63d; well, that was an all black area. I didn't have any problems when I would go through there, but when I would go through with my dad there would be hate stares. There were times I would say, 'Sorry, Dad, I'll meet you at school.' And I would walk on the other side of the street." While Lauren expressed sadness about denying her father, she also remembered the pressure she felt to toe the line. Moreover, without stable mixed-race neighborhoods, many multiracial children like Lauren were negotiating their unique circumstances alone.

Katey, a black interracially married woman in her early forties, lamented that in the 1960s and 1970s "biracial people and light-skinned blacks were used a lot" and suggested that children should be taught about the richness of blackness so they don't attempt superficial means to fit in. She explained, "Other blacks want you to prove you're black. So they have you do this that and the other thing; and, of course, you don't want to be perceived as not being black, so you do whatever strange or crazy thing that's being asked of you. I saw that happening all the time. That's another reason biracial people must have a strong foundation in their culture because they have to know that typing someone's term paper is not going to make them more black." While all African Americans have faced some version of border patrolling, multiracial and transracially adopted people face a unique form not even shared by their parents. Without access to other multiracial people, they have to be well versed in the necessary cultural capital, given the pressure exerted because of the color line.

Multiracial families that formed after the late 1970s tell a story of guarded acceptance, albeit on easier terms. This reflects both a disintegration of political unity and activism among African Americans and a broadening of the borders to include multiracial families. Angela Davis notes that "current discussions on issues around biraciality or multiple heritage have begun to problematize the notion of 'race' as an unreflected basis for community building."[22] Broadening borders have meant that multiracial families in black neighborhoods now have an easier time. For instance, for a while Christopher, a mixed-race man in his mid-twenties, was repeatedly asked to prove his blackness. He had lived with relatives in a predominantly white area for his first two years of high school, where he was never really accepted. The white students didn't accept him because he was black. The small number of black students who were bused in didn't accept him because they thought he was too white. So he decided to live with his African American mother and siblings in a predominantly black city for the final two years of high school. During the transition he felt the strongest demands to prove his blackness:

> Sometimes I'd have to prove I was black, either by fighting or by playing the dozens, things like that. Like, "I am black; I understand the language and everything." When I first got there, I had a rough time because I was coming from a predominantly white school and it's like, "What's up with the new kid? He thinks he's all that; he thinks he's white." But after about three months I fit in. The first couple months were fights, getting jumped, going to football practice and getting beat on, things like that. It was like I had to prove that I was black and I was from the neighborhood and this is why I'm here. They got over it; and ever since then, it's just been an easy ride.

Christopher still needed to prove he had the appropriate cultural capital, but once accepted he didn't need to be so careful with each action: "I would listen to rock music. Pretty soon the other guys in the weight room were listening to this music. And then it was seen as okay because by then I was accepted as black; they knew I was down."

According to Lisa Jones, unlike white neighborhoods, "black communities have always been shelter to multiethnic people."[23] While the shelter has not been granted without conditions, at least these communities have allowed for some level of acceptance. People have told me there is a level of community acceptance in black neighborhoods not found in white neighborhoods, yet all is not smooth sailing. The cool reception that some multiracial families receive is a form of border patrolling that is overtly expressed from time to time.

Lisa, an interracially married black mother living in a black neighborhood on Chicago's South Side, encountered overt hostility from a woman who called and threatened to kill her family:

> After an event at my daughter's school, about midnight, I got five phone calls from this woman. She said so many things. She said that I am selling out and called me all kinds of names and threatened to kill all of us. She left three messages on the answering machine. I had to call the police, and they told me to transcribe the calls. I was so upset that I couldn't relisten to them. She mentioned my daughter by name and said that my husband was cheating on me, and she was saying, "I'm watching you; I am watching what you do." It could have been from school. Students were asking if that [white man] was my husband, and teachers have been giving me such a hard time.

While this incident was terrifying for Lisa and her family, particularly since she has two children in grade school, she confirmed, "We have been very comfortable in the black community." Her husband, Peter, a pastor in a local church, stated, "I feel like I adopted the black community and have been adopted by the black community."

Barbara, the white mother of three multiracial children living in an "all-black south suburb" of Chicago, told me that her neighbors not only accept her but also help her out on many occasions: "After my divorce someone noticed my daughter needed a winter coat and for Christmas left one for her. There's a man up the street who acts like a father figure to my son. That sense of community is nothing I ever felt in the white community." Barbara speaks to the sense of community found in many black neighborhoods, which has developed in part through struggles against white supremacy and because blacks have turned inward for support and cultural identity. In a white-supremacist society blacks cannot count on the system working on their behalf; in fact, such a system creates life-threatening situations. Reliance on one another is necessary to survive and thrive. Once acceptance is granted, demands for proof of blackness cease— at least within a given neighborhood or community.

### Life in White Neighborhoods:
### Racism, Borderism, and the Color Line

While black neighborhoods were being simultaneously created and destroyed, the federal government was subsidizing the creation of segregated white-only suburbs. Not surprisingly, multiracial families attempting to move into white neighborhoods experience overt acts of discrimination, largely from landlords and realtors, the gatekeepers of segregation.

Realtors and landlords often come from the areas in which they are showing prospective buyers and renters. In addition to their own racism and borderism, they may fear reprisal from future clients and neighbors. Thus, some try to protect areas from any people considered outsiders.[24] In fact, until the Fair Housing Act of 1968 was passed, most multiracial families, like black families, were kept out of white areas. Once housing markets opened up, a few black and multiracial families moved to white areas in search of better housing and educational opportunities for their children. Acknowledging the pervasive institutionalized racism in the housing market, Gregory Squires notes that "access to good housing and neighborhoods, unfortunately, often means access to predominantly white or integrated areas."[25] The families move in hoping they can handle the racism.

When Candace and her husband first attempted to buy a home in a white subdivision in suburban Chicago, they feared they would be discriminated against because they were interracial. They decided her husband, David, would purchase the home because "then at least they would know it was a black person walking in." Candace recalled that she "did not see the house until [the building] was completely done. When we went to finalize the sale, the man said, 'You two think you've really pulled this off and that this is the first time we realized that you're an interracial couple. Well, we knew it before, and we had a discussion whether we wanted you in the neighborhood or not, and quite frankly we wouldn't want a lot more like you, but we will let you move in because we do have to have representatives of various nationalities and races or we'll get closed down.'"

This scenario can be interpreted in various ways. Perhaps this couple was facing borderism: intensified racism, border patrolling, and rebound racism. They were, however, allowed into the neighborhood. Thus, perhaps whites in the area found an interracial couple more palatable (more similar to themselves) than a black couple would have been. In either case, the developer's words reflected a racist ideology: whites are valued, and only a handful of others will be allowed to live among them. Such racists meet the minimum requirements of the laws so that they can maintain their privileges. These minimum requirements do little to shift historically created racial discrimination, which persists despite fair-housing legislation.

The history of post–World War II suburbanization is riddled with deliberate and conscious discrimination.[26] Squires et al. note, "Half the FHA and VA loans made during the 1950s and 1960s financed suburban housing . . . with the FHA warning of 'inharmonious racial or nationality groups,' [although] the federal government assured that properties would 'continue to be occupied by the same social and racial classes.' If redlining practices originated within the nation's financial institutions, the federal government sanctioned and reinforced such discriminatory practices at a critical time in the history of suburban development."[27] As suburbs were created, cities were drained of many resources and amenities.

The history of discrimination targeted against families of color, particularly blacks, in white neighborhoods is enough to deter many families from even attempting to locate there. The mere thought of living in such a neighborhood prompted a range of reactions from the people I interviewed. Some spoke of feeling a little scared or uncomfortable; others said they were downright terrified by the possibility of racist retaliation. Nevertheless, many multiracial families have made their way to white areas, and the fear sometimes dissipates after a family has been in a neighborhood for a while.

Parsia, a black interracially married mother who grew up in a strong black community, had many reservations before moving to a predominantly upper-class white community in Connecticut: "I was absolutely terrified. I said to my husband, 'Do you realize Connecticut has the third highest KKK membership in the nation? We can't possibly live there.

The trees go right up to the house, and the Klan could be hiding and we wouldn't see them until they were on the deck.' I had these horrible feelings about it. We had put money down on this house way out in the sticks, and I woke up in the middle of the night: 'I know it's a great house—I can't do it! It's too far from black people.' " Money was not a constraining factor when they made their housing choice: "One of the reasons we did move here is because there is a black couple across the street. Now this town has its fair share of racists, but it was the best of the alternatives. We're each within thirty minutes of work. We had to do it." Parsia reports that she is comfortable there for now. Her level of comfort may stem from the fact that her high income mediates racism. Constance Perin suggests that "differences in race and religion . . . can count not at all when the attribute of high income is also present."[28] While this means that the family can be comfortable in their home for now, Parsia expresses concern about sending her daughter to the local schools. She has plans to move to a more diverse area before her daughter begins school.

Jonathan, a white-looking biracial man, now an attorney in his late twenties, had much experience with moving into white neighborhoods. His parents, a white mother and a black father, rehabbed old homes as one source of family income. They would move into the home, fix it up, sell it, and move again. Jonathan recalled one particular move in the mid-1980s when his parents were bidding on a home in a white neighborhood: "We had a real estate agent who, without informing us, sent a letter to all the neighbors telling them that a biracial family was moving in and asking if they were going to have any problems with it. She did that because she was afraid that we were going to move in and people were just going to start doing all this hate mail and stuff. I always had mixed emotions about that because on the one hand, yes, she was doing it for us in a way, but in another way it just seemed like such a crappy thing to do." He did not want to face overt forms of racism, yet he understood that the realtor's letter represented a form of discrimination against his family.

The agent was in direct violation of the Fair Housing Act, which specifically states: "It shall be unlawful . . . to make, print, or publish . . . any notice, statement, or advertisement, with respect to the sale or rental of a dwelling that indicates any preference, limitation or discrimination based on race, color, religion, sex, handicap, familial status, national origin, or intention to make any such preference, limitation or discrimination."[29] While the act has been violated with some regularity since its inception, various fair-housing groups and advocates along with the federal government have been working on ways to track and enforce compliance. One major method for tracking discrimination in the lending field has been through the Home Mortgage Discrimination Act (HMDA). Each mortgage applicant is asked to check a racial category that best describes her or him. From this information researchers have discovered that, for instance, when blacks and whites have a similar credit history, blacks are turned down for mortgages twice as often.[30] HMDA data do reveal some good information, and several lawsuits have been won based on the collected data. The data cannot, however, account for the numbers of people who are turned away or discouraged from even filling out the application, nor does it account for those who fear discriminatory practices and thus leave the race question blank.

Recently I saw a copy of our mortgage papers. The form had several boxes for demographic information. Under *race* the bank had listed both my husband and myself as a "1." Since I knew that lenders do not keep statistics on interracial couples, I was aware that the bank had listed us as the same race. I asked the white loan officer, "What does '1' mean?"

"Oh, that just indicates that you are white," she answered.

I said, "Well, my husband is not white. Why do you have him listed as white?"

The officer replied, "Well, apparently it was left blank, so we decided based on your occupations that you must be white."

We had worked with a mortgage broker and had told him to leave the space blank because we feared discrimination. Based on the loan officer's comments, this was probably a good call. Her explanation revealed her racist and perhaps borderist understanding of the world; she believed that whites, not blacks, achieve professionally and that an interracial couple is out of the realm of possibility, particularly for two professionals.

A second method used to track discrimination is the Fair Housing Test, which detects the "difference in the quality, content, and quantity of information and service provided to potential home seekers by real estate firms, landlords and real estate agents, banks, insurance providers, and others."[31] Individuals or groups called testers are trained to present themselves in such a way that skin color, physical features, or family structure appears to be their only difference. The testers pretend to be interested in renting, buying, or obtaining a loan and take precise notes about the treatment they receive. After dozens of tests, comparisons are made, reports written, and charges filed if necessary. Multiracial families often find themselves conducting unofficial and unintentional fair-housing tests or audits in white areas. When only one partner is present, realtors and landlords assume that this person has a spouse and children of the same race.

A 1995 study by Rosenblatt et al. reports that, of the twenty-one interracial couples they interviewed in the St. Paul–Minneapolis area, only two said they had faced housing discrimination.[32] My own research indicates that most individuals either suspected they had been discriminated against or had made decisions to avoid certain areas for fear of discrimination. Several interracially married people spoke of the discrimination they had received from realtors.

Dorothy, a white interracially married mother of two, recently bought a home in Montclair, New Jersey. One Sunday afternoon, she and her husband made an appointment to drive around with a realtor to look at some homes. They pulled up in front of the real estate office, and Dorothy ran in to get a listing and meet the realtor: "I walked into the real estate office, and my husband stayed in the car. I told the agent I was looking for a house, and she gave me a map and said, 'You don't want to look on that side.' She actually said that. Then when she saw the two of us, she steered us toward the black area. She brought us to this house that was a total wreck. If you're black and white, there's an assumption that you're white trash, he's black, and they assume you don't have any money." In this case Dorothy experienced rebound racism as well as conducting an unintentional and unofficial fair-housing audit. If she and her husband had been working for a fair-housing agency, the realtor may have faced sanctions. In the eyes of this racist, essentialist, and borderist realtor, Dorothy's status as a white person had essentially changed because of her marriage to a black man. She was devalued as white trash, although his status, already devalued, did not change. The realtor kept the color line intact.

After her divorce, Ursula, the mother of one white child and three multiracial children, moved to an apartment in a predominantly white community in New Jersey. Here she encountered a landlord who committed a particularly flagrant violation of the Fair Housing Act:

> When I went to get the apartment, I went with my older son, who is white by a previous marriage. At the time we were moving in there were two girls and a bunch of kids moving in on the third floor. The landlord calls me in and says, "Come here, come here, these girls are moving in with a bunch of niggers and I didn't know." He thought my kids were with the girls upstairs. . . . He was shocked when he found out that I was the one who was moving my family in and he had said that to me. He said nothing else after that; he used to just stare at us and tried to get us evicted a couple times, and he constantly picked on us. I got tired of the kids being in that school system too. So I came to Montclair.

The landlord made it clear that he was discriminating on the basis of race and perhaps familial status. Like Dorothy, Ursula had conducted an unofficial and unintentional fair-housing test and felt the effects of rebound racism when the landlord recategorized her family as less than white. Her children's status, already devalued, did not change. Ursula's did.

While parents contend with discrimination in the process of finding housing, multiracial and transracially adopted individuals experience discrimination when they live in white areas and begin to meet neighborhood children and classmates. Several multiracial adults with whom I spoke grew up in predominantly white areas and attended white schools. Without exception, they urged parents of multiracial and transracially adopted children to find racially mixed areas to live in. Mark, a thirty-year-old mixed-race man who lived in a predominantly white community as a child, recalled, "I hung out with all white kids, and everything was fine until fifth grade. Then I guess I pissed off the wrong guy, and the whole school turned against me. Even guys who were my closest friends. Nobody spoke to me for a long time. I didn't have any friends until we moved to Montclair, which was something I couldn't believe.[33] I was coming from Bloomfield, where there were no black kids in my school, to Montclair, where there were so many different people— you know, white parents dropping off Asian children. It was great; nobody asked me anything." Mark implies that when communities are diverse, the color line loses its hold in daily life. Individuals are less likely to patrol, and overt displays of racism are ameliorated. The actual politics of race within the school and classrooms are present; but compared with living in a white area, this was a welcome relief.

Jonathan, the white-looking biracial man whose family renovated old homes, attended many different (mainly white) schools: "The pattern went something like, I'd get into a new school, kids would have no idea about me, especially before my sister got there. I'd make lots of friends. All of a sudden my parents would show up for a parent-teacher night, and I wouldn't have as many friends or any friends, depending on where the school was located, and that was really tough." Unlike Mark, who is visibly of color, Jonathan is not. He did not seem to threaten the color line until his sister or father "outed" him. His experiences highlight the ways in which the segregated housing market allows whites to ignore race—until they feel threatened by an invading outsider, and especially one, like Jonathan, whom they had previously assumed to be an insider.

When institutional forms of borderism and racism fail, individual border patrollers act out. As long as white privilege is protected through the borderism of lenders, insurers, realtors, and landlords, whites can claim a color-blind stance and avoid discussing race. This is quite different from black neighborhoods in which racial meanings are overtly contested through comparisons of skin color, hair, and other markers of belonging and authenticism. In white areas, even though Jonathan appears white, there is no way to prove that he belongs, given the appearance of his father and sister. In fact, because his appearance belies his family tree (according to racist and essentialist thinking), he may actually be held in greater suspicion.

Other multiracial adults recalled having only one close white friend or no friends at all. One terrible case is Anna, a twenty-four-year-old biracial woman who grew up in a white area in the Bronx with her white Irish mother and white siblings. She was the youngest and only child of color in her racist family; and during her entire childhood her mother repeatedly told her without further explanation that she was not African American, even though physical markers made such a conclusion ludicrous to Anna and others. Her mother's denial and her lack of interaction with other blacks left Anna confused and isolated. She recalled, "I had friends minimally as a child." In one case, she made a friend in her all-white Catholic school. When the friend's mother found out, Anna lost her only friend. Anna's mom, denying the existence of any problems, "would just never, ever do anything about it."

School itself was "horrific" because Anna felt that she was "in danger all the time. . . . There were times I did get picked on. I did fight for myself after I realized my mother wasn't going to do anything. Then I would get in trouble for fighting." She learned early in life that neither her mother nor any adult at school would stand up against the racial injustices she was facing. She learned to fight for herself. Then, much to her surprise, someone did take a stand on her behalf: "One day we were all in class, and two boys had made fun of me being a nigger and stuff like that. Very dejectedly, not believing anything in the world was going to happen, I decided, 'Well, I might as well go through protocol,' and I raised my hand. The nun flipped her lid." The two boys were strongly reprimanded in front of the entire class. For Anna, this was "the first time *ever*" that someone stood up for her. She was nine years old at the time. After this incident, the two boys never teased her again, although the treatment she received from the other students did not change.

### Racially Diverse Areas

Many arguments have been made about the need to end housing segregation and promote racially diverse areas. These arguments generally follow single-race, white, or black lines. Gunnar Myrdal and others have suggested, for instance, that whites in segregated areas are "dwarfing their minds" because they are not being exposed to cultural diversity.[34] Moreover, segregation maintained through white-controlled institutions eliminates opportunities for intergroup relations needed for a smoothly functioning society from which whites benefit disproportionately.[35] Squires et al. note that segregation creates a society in which whites do not have access, real or imagined, to housing in the entire city.[36] While whites may be inconvenienced by segregation, blacks are economically and educationally disadvantaged.[37] Many important services such as health care, libraries, and private businesses are restricted in segregated black areas.[38] Multiracial families desire racially mixed neighborhoods because there they can have a sense of safety and comfort and not face repeated acts of border patrolling and racism. The easing of border patrolling in these areas does not necessarily challenge white privilege. Living in racially mixed areas, however, does mean that border patrolling is less frantic, overt, and hostile.

After completing a five-year study of National Neighbors, an organization created to facilitate the process of housing integration, Juliet Saltman identified factors contributing to the stability of racially mixed communities, which include the presence of desirable amenities, desegregated schools, and a deconcentration of public housing.[39] Other researchers have also identified attractive and architecturally interesting housing and desirable location as important factors.[40] Amenities that help to maintain the stability of racially diverse areas (for example, parks, beaches, shopping, and access to transportation) can make these areas costly to live in. In fact, a study of fourteen stable racially diverse areas across the United States concluded that, when the communities are diverse by direction (intentionally diverse communities created through the involvement of organizations and institutions), they "are more wealthy and the community has greater professional resources."[41]

Some areas may be diverse by circumstance: racially diverse without the intervention of organizations and community organizers.[42] They tend to have more affordable housing, lower median incomes, and less political clout than do diverse-by- direction areas and thus carry the stigma of not being as stable. Without the institutionalization of diversity and given the history of hostility in changing neighborhoods, multiracial families may fear that the these areas are merely transitional. Based on my research, I found that those who cannot afford a middle-class neighborhood often opt for a single-race area rather than a working-class, racially diverse one. When they consider living in a mixed-race area, most think of middle-class, racially mixed communities that have developed the institutional and organizational networks necessary to create and maintain the diversity.[43]

When I asked, "How did you decide on the community

you live in now?" Barbara, a white mother of three living in an all-black southern suburb of Chicago, replied quickly and matter-of-factly, "I couldn't afford Hyde Park." This neighborhood, where the University of Chicago is located, is well known as a consciously developed racially mixed area. Julie, a white woman living in a white, working-class sub-urb, stated, "If I had my druthers, I'd live in Evanston, but that's very expensive." Lisa, a black interracially married mother of two living in a black neighborhood on Chicago's South Side, said, "It would be nice to be someplace that's more integrated, but I don't even know if there are any inte-grated communities that have houses we can afford at this time." These families could afford to move to the few areas that are mixed and lower income; but given the history of housing, they believe they will only find comfort and stability in diverse communities that are middle class.

Once in racially mixed areas, multiracial families lament two aspects: liberals and racist schools. Whites who move to these self-consciously planned areas are a self-selected, often liberal group. Multiracial families spoke of being sought out by members of this group. June, speaking of Montclair, New Jersey, observed, "In this town people want to show how liberal they are, so we are really sought after. It allows them to have friends of color and their children to have friends of color without them being too dark. And then you have the white mother to relate to if you are uncomfortable with African Americans. In my case, you've got this white mother—I'm acceptable."

Candace experienced a similar phenomenon in suburban Chicago: "We were the couple to know if people wanted to prove they were liberal. There was this one lady in particu-lar: she knew us when she needed us. If she was with a group of people and didn't want them to know she knew us, she wouldn't look in our direction. Other times she would come running over pell-mell. So we've either been the couple to know or not to know; we were never quite sure what the status was going to be." Multiracial families find the greatest comfort in these areas yet are confronted with a particularly troubling aspect of white liberalism in a white-supremacist society: those people who think about diversity as bean counting. In this view nothing really needs to change; it is just a matter of bringing people together and being able to claim friendships with as many African Americans and other people of color as possible. Diversity is something to be consumed, something that is exercised when convenient and discarded when privileges are threatened.[44] Clearly, this attitude does not describe all whites in racially mixed areas, but multiracial family members often perceived it.

The irritation of these parents pales in comparison with the racial problems their children face in the schools. Many point out that the schools work best for white students, who are disproportionately tracked into honors classes. Black students, on the other hand, are disproportionately tracked into general education courses. June recently joined an organization for African American parents concerned about the education system. She joined because she is the "parent of two African American boys" and became disgusted by the inequality in the school system:

> If you look at classes in the Montclair school system, the upper classes are 99 percent whites, and the lower-level courses are 100 percent black. There is not one Caucasian child in the classes. So what are they saying? It doesn't take a rocket scientist. Then you get all the whispering from white parents and teachers: "Don't you think it's the families? Don't you think it comes from the home?" Yeah, all African American kids come

from dysfunctional homes, and none of the Caucasian kids do. Let me tell you, behind some of these closed doors you would be stunned, shocked, and amazed. Our schools do a disservice to black children.

Here June highlights more than educational inequality. As a white woman, she has been privy to the behind-closed-doors discussions of other whites. This may be a primary reason why so many multiracial family members don't trust whites who claim to be liberal. According to June, many whites living in racially diverse areas want diversity on their own terms and are not concerned with institutional forms of racism. Instead, they deny racism in favor of a theory of black family dysfunction. In short, the color line and injustices are explained as an outcome inherent in the essential qualities of whiteness and blackness.

Like Montclair, Oak Park, Illinois, also has problems with racism and the educational system. Reverend Steve Saunders, a residence of Oak Park and a board member of Operation PUSH/Rainbow Coalition, says that Oak Park has a "two-tiered, white-black, gifted-remedial, apartheid-like tracking system in the high school that separates white kids from black kids. To me this is symbolic of the problems of integration, because people here are selectively concerned about exclusivity and inclusivity."[45] The good school issue is extremely sensitive in racially mixed communities, particularly in suburban schools where there is closer control of the school systems. To the multiracial families I spoke with, schools appear to work for white students who have white parents. Multiracial children and transracially adopted children with at least one white parent are given better opportunities than are students with no white parent. In fact, multiracial children are often moved into predominantly white honors classes, where they are alone or one of only a few. Black students are consistently tracked into non-college–bound or general education courses.

This difference in tracking can lead to tensions between multiracial and transracially adopted children and black children. Daphne, a bright multiracial woman who was adopted by white parents in upstate New York, was placed in her high school's upper-track classes: "By the time I got to high school, I became very militant—especially in the Catholic high school. I had to be in charge of every black organization. I had to have only black friends. It got very hard and very challenging for me because most of my classes just didn't have a whole lot of black kids in them. Like maybe one or two. Then the black kids resented me because they're like, 'Oh, your friends are white, and you live in the suburbs.' And the white kids—I never felt like I fit with them." She admits that her militancy was about trying to fit in, yet institutional forms of discrimination continued to separate her from black students who didn't have white parents. These difficulties may be exacerbated by a suspicion that these multiracial and transracially adopted children are being counted as black for purposes of school statistics. In short, a buffer group is created even as individuals like Daphne struggle against racist injustice. Reflecting on her educational experience she acknowledges that, while it may have been difficult, at least she was given the opportunity to succeed that was denied to other African American children.

### The Importance of Racially Mixed
### Areas for Racially Mixed Families

Despite the many difficulties of living in racially mixed areas, multiracial and transracially adopted adults emphasize that parents should find housing in stable racially mixed areas. So much is tied to the area in which one lives.

This is particularly true for children who are developing a sense of themselves in the world.[46] When parents and children think about the neighborhood in which they live, they see it from different vantage points. While parents may be concerned about safety, property values, quality of schools, and accessibility to work, children are concerned about other children in the neighborhood and their experience in school. Parents generally leave the neighborhood for their workplace. They have coworkers and friends outside the neighborhood. If they happen to live someplace where neighbors interact, this often involves no more than the exchange of small favors. Yet the children's world often starts and ends in the neighborhood—attending neighborhood schools and playing with other children close to home. Children's self-esteem, identity, and interaction with others who can affirm their experiences are bound to the place their parents call home.

Katey, an African American, interracially married mother and president of a multiracial organization on Long Island, stated, "Being in an interracial neighborhood is the number one thing that you need because people I've talked with who had problems growing up biracial have grown up in monoracial neighborhoods. White or black, it doesn't matter: monoracial." Of course, given the borderism, racism, and classism in the housing market, affordable and stable racially diverse areas are not easy to find. Moreover, parents do not always understand the problems their children will face in the neighborhoods and schools.

What may feel perfectly comfortable to an adult may be very difficult for a child. For instance, Oscar, a white interracially married father of three grown mixed-race sons, thought of the Lower East Side of Manhattan as an easy place to live: "We lived on the Lower East Side and really stayed in the same neighborhood that has always been mixed. In the sixties and seventies it was a big hippie hangout, but it's been a neighborhood where anyone can live. You're not really breaking any barriers." In fact, the Lower East Side has always provided a haven for people who do not conform to social norms. This was where the beat movement developed in New York City and where beat poet and cultural critic Leroi Jones (Amiri Baraka) and Heddy Jones lived as a multiracial family. Nevertheless, when I spoke with Kimberly, a mixed-race woman who grew up in Brooklyn and attended high school on the Lower East Side in the late 1970s and early 1980s, her recollections were not quite as glowing: "I went to a high school where the black people went out the front and the white people went out the other side of the building. So if you identified yourself with people of color, you went out that side of the building. If you identified with another group of people, you went out the other side and hung out there." I asked her which door she chose, and she joked, "I stood in the middle turning in circles." In reality, she had a mixed group of friends. By choosing friends from many backgrounds, she reduced the pressure of border patrolling in daily interaction. The color line became distanced, muted.

Vincent, a racially mixed man who grew up in the Robert Taylor Homes in Chicago, recalled that throughout high school he left his racially segregated community and headed toward the racially mixed area of Hyde Park: "I felt there were people I could talk to and identify with. It was funny because that was the only place I could go and feel comfortable. There were some nice people there, and they always listened to what I said and how I was being treated, and they would let me know that I was going to be okay." He found relief by traveling to a racially mixed community. For multiracial families who can afford to live there, Hyde Park provides a haven in an otherwise racially divided and hostile city—a space for multiracial families interested in urban living to feel comfortable. Mary, a thirty-year-old mixed-race woman who grew up in Hyde Park, described it as "a very liberal mixed-race world." Growing up and going to school "was really no big deal. Everyone was just like me. My best friend was white, and all my other friends were mixed. It was never any big deal to have all different kinds of friends because Hyde Park was all mixed." Unfortunately for many multiracial families, Hyde Park, like many racially mixed areas, remains out of reach due to its high cost of housing.

Most interracially married parents have grown up in single-race communities. By the time they have children and move to a racially mixed area, they have faced a great deal of borderism. White interracial parents spoke of the discomfort they felt when they had to leave their racially mixed neighborhood with their children. These parents often think of multiracial areas as havens of safety and comfort, and many fear traveling outside of the area. For all Montclair's problems June is not comfortable leaving the town with her children: "I'm not that brave. I don't go to Bloomfield. I feel very comfortable in this town. We went to get a Christmas tree this year, and the boys wanted to stop to get a bite to eat, and I suddenly found myself in a town I didn't know, and I was getting very scared. I was very uptight because I didn't know what would happen."

Once a family has lived in an area for a while, they understand the rules that guide racial interactions; they get a feel for the color line as it is enacted in their area. Visiting a new place risks new or different rules, and many parents fear they will trip on the color line and their children will be physically or emotionally harmed. Mina told me, "Every time we leave Montclair, I get very nervous. I'm getting used to it, but I have that fear. Like someone could not see us for who we are and act out against us. We are safe on our street, and we knew we would be when we moved in."

Unfortunately for multiracial families in racially mixed areas, that fear can make their world isolated. The color line and borderism keep these families in check. White mothers from multiracial areas spoke disproportionately of this fear, perhaps because they discovered the terror of racism later in life and had not yet developed strategies for coping with it. Moreover, the subtleties of race, a social construct, vary from one geographic location to another. Rules of acceptable behavior and interactions shift.

## Conclusion

The housing market protects white privilege by strengthening the color line. Discrimination in the housing market has created geographically defined racial spaces that are then translated into an actual color line. The pervasiveness of redlining in the mortgage and insurance industries tells the story, as does the lack of stable racially mixed neighborhoods.[47] The few racially diverse communities that do exist have their own set of problems inextricably linked to the dual-housing market and the larger racist society. Within the context of the housing market, then, the color line seems essential and clear. Yet a look at the lives of multiracial family members in a racially divided world shows us that the color line is constantly under construction.

# 3

## We Are the

## Nation's

## Racial

## Rorschach

## Tests

A Rorschach test analyzes how an individual responds to and interprets an abstract ink stain. The way in which people make sense of these stains helps explain how they identify themselves in the world. Thus, the beauty of the test is its ambiguity.

Identities are strongly tied to personal relationships with the world, which is defined through categories and boundaries.[1] Human bodies are interpreted and explained as they might be with a Rorschach test. Some bodies easily match a category's description and appear simple to interpret; others are more ambiguous. Sometimes the body is not ambiguous; but politics, culture, family, and ways of being make categorization difficult. Our physical bodies mediate our experiences in the world and are used from birth to place us into particular categories.[2] Categories defined by status and stereotype guide social interactions among individuals. When these categories are challenged, so are personal identities.

When people encounter a racially ambiguous person, they conduct a flurry of analyses to determine how the individual should be categorized. This is a racial Rorschach test, taken in a society that creates and accepts racial stereotypes. Interpretations develop within a cultural, social, and historical context and, like all interpretations, depend on the language available to frame ideas. Michael Omi and Howard Winant suggest that "analyzing stereotypes reveals the always present, already active link between our view of the social structure—its demography, its laws, its customs, its threats—and our conceptions of what race means."[3] Racial stereotypes become apparent as essentialist thinkers share their interpretations of racially ambiguous people. The more limited the ways in which individuals understand race, the more likely they are to cling to racial stereotypes and demand that others remain "in accordance with their racial formula, to follow the script."[4] Clothes, hair, street address, familial ties, musical preferences, friendship networks, politics, and manner of speech are all quickly assessed.[5] Once a determination is made about where this ambiguous person belongs, judgments and demands often follow. The racially ambiguous person is expected to adhere to a set of racial codes. Individuals who cannot or will not comply face a multitude of responses ranging from degradation to congratulation.

In "Race As Process: Reassessing the "What Are You?' Question," Teresa Kay Williams notes that members of multiracial families "are not mere receivers of social messages or conformists to prescriptive racial categories. They are also active participants in shaping their identities and creating social reality."[6] In other words, unlike ink blots, human beings do not passively wait to be interpreted and categorized. They actively respond. In the process of interaction, individuals are challenged to transcend simplistic understandings of race. At the same time, the color line is being created, challenged, and transformed.

People often see what they want to see, what they are comfortable seeing, what they are trained to see. What some are able to see is more sophisticated than what others can see. Racially ambiguous people are generally forced to think about race in more sophisticated ways, beyond essentialism. During interactions, they spend energy and time deciphering others' levels of racial knowledge. Daphne, for instance, has found that "there is such an overwhelming need to stick you in a box; and if there's no one else in the box, they don't know how to act towards you. If they can't deal with it, they end up putting you in one of the other two boxes, and then they deal with you on whatever level they can." This need "to stick you in a box" arises in a society in which racial categories, assumed to be genetic or biological, mediate interactions. Daphne is interpreted racially; in turn, she interprets how others interpret her, searching for clues to their levels of racial understanding and the meaning of race in society.

Interactions between multiracial family members and essentialist thinkers provide insight about how the color line is constructed and reinforce the connection between the color line and the protection of white privilege and power. Moreover, because blackness cannot be reduced to skin color and the struggle against whiteness, border patrolling among African Americans highlights the complex and dynamic aspects of blackness. This chapter primarily considers the experiences of mixed-race people and white interracially married people who do not claim a white identity to show how the color line is both challenged and reproduced through daily interactions.

## Insights into Essentialist Thinking

Everyone who has learned about race, American style, looks for clues about how to racially categorize others. Some whites need to take this step before they feel comfortable interacting with new people. They may sense that the color line is shifting and fear losing their racial status. Thus, until they can categorize others, they feel vague and uneasy about their own racial status and identity.[7] For people of color, the desire to distinguish the color line may concern a quest for allegiance and unity, a means to determine who is "us" and who is "them" politically, socially, and culturally.

Most people do not go out of their way to make multiracial family members uncomfortable. They may not like, approve of, or understand what they see; but except for making irritating comments and staring, few act out physically. More often people act in ways they believe are polite and appropriate. Nonetheless, people react. Carla Bradshaw notes in "Beauty and the Beast: On Racial Ambiguity" that "regardless of the character of the response, the mixed-race individual seldom fails to evoke some response."[8] Similarly, when people unexpectedly discover that a person is from a mixed family, they respond.

Generally, single-race family networks are taken for granted, particularly by whites. When multiracial families are together in public, observers often assume they are unrelated. For example, it is common for a restaurant hostess to ask one family member, "How many people are in your party?" and then turn to another member and ask the same question. This may happen even when the family is talking together. Such incidents are repeated in most public spaces, including the school system.

Ursula, the white mother of three grown mixed-race children recalled, "I went in for a conference for Davina, and the teacher said, 'Julie is doing really great this year!'

"I said, 'Who the hell is Julie?'

"He said, 'You are Mrs. So and So aren't you?'

"I'm like, 'No, I'm Davina's mother.'

" 'Oh, I'm sorry; let me get her file.' "

Laughing, Ursula said, "He was amazed. I guess I did not fit the picture he had painted."

Similarly, June, the white mother of two biracial sons, told me, "When I went for Segal's conference this year, there were four teachers sitting there. When I walked into the room, they looked at me and said, 'Can we help you? Are you lost?'

"I said, 'I don't think so.'

" 'Oh! Come sit down!' They couldn't get up fast enough to shake my hand." She laughed at the discomfort these teachers must have felt as they tripped over the color line.

Both Ursula and June live in diverse communities in which multiracial families are more common, yet the teachers still did not make the connection. The assumption that families are single race is overwhelming in the United States—and is of little surprise given that the color line has been constructed around the definition of a pure white family.[9]

The daily struggles of multiracial family members show how the color line is created through individual and institutional means and then made to appear natural. For instance, families have difficulty locating resources such as books, dolls, toys, and cards with multiracial themes. This lack of resources reflects the threat that multiracialism poses to an essentialist color line. Candace, the white interracially married mother of five recalled, "When our kids were growing up, it was hard to find books that reflected mixed-race families. I had to sit and color cards myself, and I wrote some of my own stories for the kids so they'd have stuff to read." Katey, the black interracially married mother of a ten-year-old biracial daughter, remarked, "I was in the bookstore the other day and saw a book on raising black children and thought, 'Why can't we have this—one measly book.' " As if in answer, a card company now exists to cater to multiracial families, several magazines address this community, and a few companies carry multicultural books, toys, dolls, and games. Unfortunately these products rarely appear at local stores—not because there is no market but because businesses may fear offending those who believe that individuals who are essentially, racially different should not mix. Candace Malstrom, owner of Colorblind Creations Card Company, which produces special-occasion cards for multiracial families, has reported that some retailers "liked the cards personally, but didn't display them for fear of offending customers."[10] Candy Mills, editor of *Interrace Magazine*, writes, "sadly, many advertisers believe 'Interracial' couples and families are too controversial" and thus will not purchase advertisements in the magazine.[11]

Nevertheless, advertisers continue to feature endless numbers of multiracial children, adults, and couples in their advertisements. The use of multiracial actors is part of the colorism common in a white-supremacist society. Light-skinned blacks, whom whites view as more acceptable than darker-skinned blacks, appear in commercials and movies so that advertisers can seem more inclusive. Multiracial children and adults, especially those with visibly mixed features, are often portrayed as having two African American parents. In short, rather than sell resources directly to multiracial

people and families, companies exploit and exoticize multiracialism with the goal of selling products.

African Americans continue to struggle with colorism.
Historically (and continuing into the present), lighter skin
and straighter hair raised one's status in the black community. W.E.B. Du Bois's Talent Tenth—a list of those who
would lead the black community to liberation—consisted of
"twenty-one men and two women, all but one of whom were
mulatto."[12] Beginning in the slave era, mulattos and lighter-
skinned blacks were given easier access to education and
employment opportunities. In *The Color Complex: The Politics of Skin Color among African Americans*, Kathy Russell and her colleagues tell us that "in a society that is
politically and economically controlled by whites, those
members of minorities with the lightest skin and the most
Caucasian-looking features have been allowed the greatest
freedom."[13] Thus, by "selling" multiracial actors as black,
advertisers avoid confronting essentialism and racism and
maintain the color line that privileges people with light
skin and European features.

## The Pride of Blackness

While whites have controlled the parameters of public race discussions to make race appear simplistic and natural, blacks have maintained a broader sense of blackness,
one that includes a claimed and constructed cultural identity. Manning Marable notes, "When African Americans
think about blackness, we usually are referring to . . . racial
identity, a category the Europeans created and deliberately
imposed on us for the purpose of domination, and black
cultural identity, which we constantly reinvent and construct
for ourselves. . . . Blackness to [many white Americans] is

skin color and a person's physical features period."[14] Black identity is broader than just skin color and physical features. Thus, black border patrolling takes place within the continuing creation of cultural identity. In "Mulatto Millennium," Danzy Senna says, "You told us all along that we had to call ourselves black because of this so-called one drop. Now that we don't have to anymore, we choose to. Because black is beautiful. Because black is not a burden, but a privilege."[15] Blacks feel a sense of affirmation when other blacks accept them as black.

In *From Black to Biracial*, Kathy Odell Korgen suggests that multiracial people do not identify themselves as white because "it is still not acceptable for a biracial person who appears white to identify racially as white."[16] Yet acceptable or not, most multiracial people (and in some cases their white parents) choose to claim identities other than white because of a sense of pride, affirmation, and political solidarity with people of color. In fact, multiracial people who are not readily accepted as black by other blacks may feel hurt. This is particularly true of those who appear white. Jonathan, a white-looking biracial man who grew up in white neighborhoods, explained, "I always bring up that I'm half black, and the standard response is 'No, you're kidding,' or 'No, not really.' I don't blame people if they don't see me as black because I don't look it; but after I tell you, I want you to accept it. I am not making a joke of this. I've been through a lot of shit, and at least I deserve to be recognized for what I say I am. I carry around a picture of my family so I can say, 'Do you want to see a picture of my family?' I do that before they get a chance to say, 'You're not really black' and the 'Are you adopted?' crap."

Because Jonathan looks white and has lived in white neighborhoods and attended white schools his entire life, his cultural capital—his mannerisms and references—often belies his claimed racial identity. Life might be easier for him if he would stop showing his family picture and live as a white person in the world, something he has considered from time to time. Yet his discomfort at not having others recognize him as black does not outweigh his sense of solidarity with his "father, sister and other African Americans." Unfortunately, without a sense of connection to other African Americans, he feels isolated. His parents were not involved in any black organizations because they felt rejected by the black community. As a result, Jonathan has had little contact with other blacks. He may be black according to definitions set forth by whites, yet he lacks a connection to blackness as a cultural and social experience.[17]

Jessie also appears white to most people. Unlike Jonathan, however, she grew up in a black neighborhood in Brooklyn with her Jewish mother and her West Indian father and claimed a black identity until her mid-twenties. At that time she changed her language: "I became decidedly mixed race. It was just easier; I didn't feel like an imposter." Her cultural identity is black, although her body does not mark her in that way. Because of her features, Jessie has not faced racist abuse to the same degree that darker-skinned blacks do. She fears that claiming to be black will insult those who have suffered greatly because of racist abuses: "I have never really been directly challenged by a black person. No one had ever said anything insulting to make me feel unwelcome, but many black people don't know I'm black. It's not my fault I don't look black, but black people don't see me as black; I just have to admit that." After much pain, she has come to terms with this fact but still wears "bracelets that could mark me as West Indian" and does "slip into Black English." By changing what she calls herself racially and assuming certain racial markers, Jessie is challenging the basic idea that race is essential and static. Unfortunately, many blacks hear the term *mixed race* and assume that she is trying to escape blackness, a reaction that may move her away from the connections she seeks.

Light-skinned multiracial people often desire darker skin so that they will not be mistaken for white. Although such a mistake can provide a social and economic boost in a racist society, it can also lead to loneliness. Several multiracial women prayed that their unborn children would have dark skin so that they wouldn't always have to proclaim their blackness. Kimberly, who has light skin and racially ambiguous features, shared her dreams for the future: "I have to say I hope I end up marrying a black man so my daughter has darker skin than me and she knows she's black, so she has the appearance and a background. I think that sometimes, and then other times I think I should marry whomever I deem worthy, regardless of color." Lauren, now age forty-two, used to share Kimberly's sentiments: "When I was pregnant with my daughter, I prayed every night that she would not have to answer questions. I was so grateful that she was brown and her hair was nappy and she is obviously African American." Silvia, who has blue eyes and light-brown hair, recently married a white man and is struggling with the same issue: "I really didn't care what color the person was that I fell in love with, but I wanted my kids to be black. I want my kids to have the benefit of their black heritage because we [white-looking black people] are not seen as black by a lot of people, so we're not seen as sharing in the whole black history. I want my kids to know about all the civil rights activities of my father and grandfather, but I also want everyone else to know that we are part of that, that whole history, but it's kind of hard when you don't have the skin color."

The idea of black as a privilege is something most whites have difficulty understanding. As Manning Marable points out, blackness "is a cultural and ethnic awareness we have collectively constructed for ourselves over hundreds of years."[18] My research reflects that multiracial people and their families desire a connection to blackness. This does not mean that an extended white family is rejected or that white ethnic backgrounds are belittled; rather, culturally, politically, and socially, these people would prefer to share in the creation of blackness. Their desire for a connection to blackness runs contrary to the racist thinking of many whites, who firmly believe that all people of color wish for whiteness.

### "I'll Always Think of You As White" and Other Racist Compliments

For racist and essentialist thinkers, whiteness implies inherent values and points of superiority. Thus, many whites assume that people of color covet their whiteness. Multiracial family members, however, often challenge this assumption that white is a compliment and black an insult. For instance, whites often ask white mothers of multiracial or black children if they have adopted the children—a way of explaining away disturbing issues of racial identity and power. As Candace lamented, "So many people ask, 'Are these your adopted children?' The kids get so mad when people say, 'Is that your mom? How can that be?' And we look alike, but people don't look for that. I had one woman tell me, 'You left your baby out in the sun too long!'

" 'No, that's his color.'

" 'Is your husband Italian?'

" 'No.' "

As you can see, whites attempt to explain away Candace's familial ties so that she fits neatly into the white category.

Julie, like other interracial parents, has faced the adoption question everywhere, including the grocery store: "I was at the store, and this lady said, 'What a beautiful baby. Is she yours?'

"I said, 'Yes.'

" 'Did you adopt her?'

"I said, 'No, I had her the old-fashioned way. Blacks and whites can have children; we're not separate species.'

"And she said, 'I wasn't, I mean, I wasn't, I didn't, I wasn't!' She was not being nasty. She was just stupid! No one would ever ask a white woman if her white baby is hers." Julie shook her head, laughed slightly, then sighed. The woman in the store, like so many others, never considered other possibilities.

Ingrid, a white interracially married adoptive mother, also faces the adoption question. She is ambivalent about how she should handle it. Ingrid's husband is black; thus, any biological children would have been mixed, as their adopted daughter is. Ingrid identifies herself as an interracially married mother. She is no longer a play-by-the-rules good white woman. If others know only that her daughter is adopted, the color line remains unchallenged, leaving Ingrid to look like a "good white woman" who hasn't been polluted by interracial sex.[19] Within this context the adoption question becomes a racist compliment.

Multiracial people face another form of racist compliment: "I'll always think of you as white." Jessie recalled an incident that occurred when she was learning to drive:

> I had a driving instructor who was a racist. He was going on with this constant racism, and I had this passing anxiety. I felt like I was passing: this man had no idea I was black. I was in this car with him, and I didn't feel safe, but I wanted to learn how to drive. But I also felt ashamed that I was passing, so I decided to say something the next time he opened his mouth. He started,

and I said, "I have to tell you my father is black, and I don't want you to talk this way anymore."

He was shocked, and it was obvious he liked me, so this was very confusing to him. He actually said, "Well, I don't think of you as a black person. I can tell you're just like a white person. And everyone has something in their past they're not comfortable with."

So I explained to him, "No, it's not a skeleton in my closet; it's something I'm very proud of."

The instructor saw whiteness as something valuable, something to be cherished. He disdained blackness. He had been addressing Jessie as an equal—as a white. Thus, after discovering her "secret," he needed to create a facade to ease his discomfort. By thinking of her as white, he attempted to explain his racist sense of superiority and his inability to distinguish what he perceived as an essential difference. Neil Gotanda suggests that the construction of race and white supremacy becomes clear in the moment of discovering that an individual is not white:

> Before the moment of recognition, white acquaintances may let down their guard, betraying attitudes consistent with racial subordination, but which whites have learned to hide in the presence of nonwhites. Their meeting and initial conversation were based on the unsubordinated equality of white-white relationship, but at the moment of racial recognition the exchange is transformed into a white-black relationship of subordination. In that moment of recognition lies the hidden assertion of white racial purity.[20]

For many whites, questioning race means questioning their internalized notions of superiority. By making an exception to the rule and thinking of Jessie as white, the driving instructor avoided thinking about race on a more complex level and was able to maintain his racist and essentialist stereotypes. Like this man, many whites think they can bestow the honor of whiteness onto people of color. "I can tell that you're just like a white person" is meant to be a compliment, a way of saying, "I'm willing to overlook your flaw; I'm willing to see you as an equal." In turn, the person of color is supposed to feel flattered and grateful.

The racist compliment, grounded in the devaluation of blackness, takes another form: condolences based on the assumption that a multiracial family member is ashamed of his or her connection to blackness. One evening when I was in graduate school, I was talking with a group of European women. One woman whom I did not know began asking about my research. I told her about it, my family, and multiracialism in general. At the end of our conversation she reached over, touched me, and said, "Thank you for sharing. I know that must have been hard." I almost choked. Was she was implying that I had just shared a terrible secret? All I managed to say was "It wasn't hard at all."

Ingrid recalled a time when a stranger approached her and her mixed-race daughter in a mall and sympathized, "It's okay, you know. I'm divorced. . . . My husband used to beat me." The message, of course, was that they were exchanging shameful secrets. For many whites, this idea of a revealed secret is tied to the belief that mixed-race people want to pass for white and that interracially married whites want to hide their family but have instead been found out. In *Bulletproof Diva*, Lisa Jones, a self-identified black woman born to a white Jewish mother and a black father, writes about how she and friends joke about "whites' inability to imagine why we would want to see ourselves as people of color and as African Americans—how connected this makes us feel.

What could they possibly think is *in it* for us to be white people?"[21]

Many whites don't see the pride of blackness because they believe that black is not desirable. Jonathan, a white-looking mixed-race man, shared how this concept was relayed to him: "One of the administrators at Northwestern [University] came to me and said, 'Jonathan, can I have a word with you?' When I got to her office, she said, 'I'm afraid we've made a horrible mistake.' (I always remember that: '"a horrible mistake.') 'We have you marked down as black.'

"I said, 'Well, I am. It's true.' "

He laughed. "She's like, 'Oh, okay, great, well, then, we haven't made a mistake!' " Still laughing, he continued: "I said, 'That's it?' and she said, 'Well, yes. I'm glad you're here at Northwestern, congratulations.' "

## Responding to Essentialist and Racist Interpretations

Multiracial family members like Lauren feel they have an obligation to "correct whites very firmly" when they demonstrate preconceived notions about the value of whiteness versus blackness. Some spy on whites and then speak out against racist perspectives. Many others, however, tire of this response and just let essentialist assumptions slide.

### Spying

Both white-looking multiracial people and white interracial parents and partners are besieged with racist compliments. Thus, they are constantly thinking about how and when to come out. Many take the opportunity to spy on unsuspecting whites and then, like Danzy Senna, "report back to headquarters."[22] Because of the relatively low percentage of intermarriage and a general lack of awareness that white-looking black people exist, whites often assume they are "among their own" when they are around others who appear white. June, the white mother of two biracial sons, told me, "You live with that awkward feeling of being a spy. The scariest thing for me is that [white] people are so sure of the racism that they don't mind coming up to a perfect stranger and talking about 'niggers this or that.' They just assume everybody thinks the way they do. So you feel like you almost have to wear a button that says, 'I am not white.' " She laughed, then paused to search for words. "I mean, obviously I know I'm white, but I'm not white." June belongs to an organization of African American parents concerned about their children's educational experience. This, combined with the fact that she has curly, dark-brown hair, has led her to hope that some people might think she is a light-skinned African American.

Being seen as "one of us" among whites does have advantages beyond accessing privileges granted to whites. It allows for spying—educating and challenging essentialist and racist thinkers. Vanessa, a mixed-race woman, uses her racially ambiguous features to spy on and then challenge racists: "Being the complexion I am, especially if my hair is straight, [white] people will open their mouths and talk, talk, talk, and I'll sit there and make them feel stupid—open their eyes. I feel like a spy sometimes because their perception of me is totally different and then they see and it's too late." In "Mulatto Millennium," Danzy Senna explains that her ambiguous features mean that whites often think of her as white. After sitting in a room with whites and listening to them talk about "colored folks," she might "spring it on them, tell them who [she] really was, and watch, in a kind of pained glee, as their faces went from eggshell white, to rose pink, to hot mama crimson, to The Color Purple."[23] Each of these women challenges essentialist understandings of race. The glee Senna speaks of comes from knowing that she has undermined the taken-for-granted essentialist color line. Racist and essentialist whites are being told take notice that race is more than physical appearance.

### Letting It Slide: Playing with Essentialism

In 1948 Walter White wrote, "I am a Negro. My skin is white, my eyes are blue, my hair is blond. The traits of my race are nowhere visible upon me."[24] As a white-looking black man, he risked his life to investigate lynchings in the South. In Arkansas in 1920, he narrowly escaped being lynched himself by catching the next train out of town. On his way to the train a white man told him, "You're leaving, mister, just when the fun is going to start. . . . There's a damned yellow nigger down here passing for white and the boys are going to get him."[25] White let this man's assumption slide. In this case, letting it slide (or passing) was a matter of life and death—and not only for him. The lives of thousands of blacks rested on the outcome of his investigations.

Today the stakes are rarely so immediate or high, yet many multiracial family members let racist and essentialist assumptions go without correction. Each time a family member faces a comment or situation that is in obvious need of a more sophisticated understanding, he or she must decide if it is worth the time and energy to respond. When multiracial family members let it slide, they give a tacit nod of agreement to essentialist ideas. Their silence on behalf of multiracial family members reinforces the color line. Yet people may let it slide for several reasons, including a belief that some people are not open enough to think through race on a more sophisticated level. They may be tired of explaining. They may lack the language or understanding to explain race to others. In some cases, they may have economic, social, or political reasons. For example, when attending to business in single-race groups, they may find that speaking about their multiracial family is a hindrance. Some choose to address acts of racism rather than essentialism. Others choose which essentialist expressions to address. In specific situations, they may prefer to let single-race assumptions slide—for example, a black association meeting or a predominantly white town meeting as well as when a family member is among a group of borderists.

The Black Association. In some cases, black interracially married people do not reveal that they are a member of a multiracial family for fear of reprisal from family, friends, or black business associates. For example, Parsia does not bring her white husband to some professional events or mention the racial makeup of her family because these facts may get in the way of other business: "For club events like the National Black MBA Association or things of that sort, I haven't taken my husband because I think it's blacks gathering to give advice, promote, and network with other blacks. I think the fact that I'm in an interracial relationship would be more disruptive than not, so I've chosen not to bring him to a race-specific kind of club." She acknowledges the need for black Americans to connect with one other. In other words, although the community boundaries are hurtful to multiracial families, they are necessary in a white-supremacist society. Without a connection to other black MBAs, Parsia risks negotiating in white corporate America without the support and sense of connection she receives from other blacks. Although she told me she would never overtly deny her family, she does let essentialist assumptions slide in her business life; she makes a tacit denial.

The White Town Meeting. Many interracially married whites and white-looking multiracial people say that other whites dismiss them once these whites learn they are part of a multiracial family. Mina, an interracially married white mother living in Montclair, New Jersey, explained why she will not bring her husband or son to a town meeting: "They already have problems with me because I am one of the leaders of a group opposing some landscaping projects. If they saw that I was interracially married, then they would peg me as a raving revolutionary liberal, and I think it would be uncomfortable to walk in with my husband because I already know their attitudes." In this case, Mina passes because she does not want to lose negotiating power in a predominantly white situation. By allowing others to assume she is from a white family, she is negotiating within a system in which whites who cross the color line are deemed pariahs. She has retained her option to be accepted as white, something people of color can never do and something other whites in interracial families choose not to do. Interestingly, Mina lives in a diverse town in which many multiracial families find some level of comfort. Yet even here they sometimes find it best to let essentialist and racist assumptions slide.

### Approaching a Racial Lesson

Most multiracial people feel responsible for educating borderists. They also acknowledge that doing so can be tiring and stressful, particularly when they are addressing people who do not want to hear them. Social justice and racial inequality become central concerns when people decide how to respond to borderists. Many multiracial family members spoke of distinguishing between personal attacks based on stereotypical thinking and attacks directed at institutional productions of racist power. Speaking of conversations with blacks, Nancy, a biracial attorney in Chicago, explained, "I don't like personal attacks. If comments are about the glass ceiling for blacks, I won't say anything because that is there; but if it's 'don't trust whitey,' well, I'm sitting there thinking, 'don't trust my mom?' 'don't trust my relatives?' Then I might speak up." As Nancy suggests, responding to borderists requires a level of sophisticated racial thought: she has identified institutional racism as a rallying point against which blacks can unify as distinct from the essentialist rally against all white people.

Many multiracial family members also distinguish between the way in which they respond to black versus white border patrolling. Lauren, a multiethnic woman, suggested, "I tend to correct whites very firmly, more firmly than I correct blacks. I don't go out of my way to correct black people, but I definitely go out of my way to correct white people. That probably comes from the perception that white people find light-skinned blacks less threatening or somehow more acceptable, and I don't want them to find me acceptable because of who they think I am." In each of these cases, race as power is central to the decision to respond.

Among those who have the time and energy to educate essentialist thinkers, the question of how to do so becomes central. Sometimes they let comments slide and then approach individuals later outside the group setting. They may also prepare people ahead of time. Many individuals think of how to let others know about their multiracial family so that borderist questions and reactions can be fielded in advance. Thus, these family members can choose the arena in which they educate others, working actively, consciously, and more comfortably to transform the color line.

### Educating in Private

Daphne agrees that the arena in which she approaches people who have made borderist comments is central to how she will be received: "I try to deal with things tactfully because it wouldn't do me any good to stand up at a lunch table and say, 'That's such a stupid thing to say.' I was annoyed with a comment this man made at lunch the other day, but I didn't berate him in front of the whole group, but I did approach him later and said, 'Do you understand why what you said was inappropriate?' " Owen, a black interracially married man living in Oak Park, Illinois, explained that he does not "get on a soapbox" unless he is directly asked about multiracialism. He noted, however, that the arena must be appropriate, or the individual might not be receptive. A group is one arena that Owen and others agree does not work: "It might be better to get a person away from the group so he or she will listen. If you say it in a group, everyone will hear it, and then they will be influenced by the fact that it's being said in front of a group. So they might not be in the best mood to receive what I have to say, so why say it at all if you're not going to get through?" Race is emotionally charged, and many fear that publicly reprimanding or educating someone will only cause them to become embarrassed and angry. In private, individuals may be more open to questioning their racial thinking without fearing they've been publicly labeled a sellout or a racist. I heard repeatedly from multiracial family members interested in educating others that if someone is going to be open enough to listen, we should not attack them. The reverse also holds true: if we attack, particularly in public, they will surely not listen. All of this takes a great deal of planning and mental and emotional energy.

### Preparing Ahead of Time

Multiracial family members often find they can effectively educate or diffuse borderists by prepping them— actively approaching people with essentialist or racist assumptions. Rather than waiting for others to figure out that the color line has been crossed, the family member chooses to address multiracialism on his or her own terms at an opportune moment, before introducing other members of the family.

Concern for one's family is the primary reason for prepping coworkers, bosses, and acquaintances. Such concerns may include fears that essentialists will say something hurtful, embarrassing, and racist or that multiracialness will overshadow an entire interaction. For example, Candace, a white interracially married mother and teacher, preps coworkers so that her family does not have to deal with inquisitions or awkward silences: "If I knew my kids or my husband were coming to the school to get me, I might tell [the people I work with], the principal, or say something to somebody because I wouldn't have wanted them to have an ugly experience of being pushed out the door." Likewise, Parsia considers both her husband's and her business associates' feelings and makes a point to explain her interracial marriage before an introduction:

> I prepare people beforehand because I don't want to show up and have them feel off guard. I usually try to have a lunch beforehand: "You know, we're going to be at this event, yeah, I'm bringing Joe, dah, dah, dah, and—you know Joe is white, right?" Or a lot of times we'll be talking about our families, and I'll say, "I went to synagogue," and they'll go, "Huh?" "Oh, yeah, my husband is Jewish; he's white." I introduce the concept so they have a chance to say, "Really?" or "Wow!" Just so they don't have to deal with it on the spot because I don't want it to be uncomfortable for them or him, especially if it's a situation where we're trying to get business done, because I feel it would just get in the way.

Quisha, a black interracially married mother, said, "Maybe it's wrong to do, but I still prep people because I hate awkward silences and I think I can deal with it better one on one. I'd rather just deal with it in my own way and just prepare them. . . . At work I put a picture of my husband on my desk, and it's like, 'Oh, who's that?' 'Oh that's my husband.' Or like tanning comes up, and I'll say, 'Yeah, Raymond always turns bright red; it's that Irish in him,' and no one ever follows up with that, but you can tell it's like, ching, ching, ching, ching." While Quisha has thought through how she wants to introduce her white spouse to others, she is still uncertain about whether this is the best approach. "Maybe it's wrong to do" reflects the uncertainty of life across the color line, where prescribed racial rules do not exist.

Rather than conversing, many people choose to display pictures of family members. Most often these pictures sit on desks, allowing people to inquire or silently think about what they see. Jonathan carries pictures to prove he is half black, Quisha keeps her husband's picture on her desk, Joe carries around his daughter's picture, and Ingrid hangs a picture on her office wall. Lisa has decided to carry a picture of her family and place one on her desk: "There is a picture on my desk at school; that's the easiest way to tell them. Maybe it will kind of hit them softly if they see the picture first on my desk or in my wallet and see that I am at ease, that this is my family." Pictures are one way to avoid having to think about how to introduce the concept. Yet they sometimes beg questions that the family member may not want to contend with at a given time.

### This Is Humorous, but It Is Not a Joke

When multiracial family members tire of being diplomatic, they sometimes use humor as a way to educate—

and as a way to trip on and have fun at the expense of essentialist thinkers. Many believe that racism and borderism are so pervasive that there is no hope for educating "stick to your own" people through a serious discussion. Shocking them through humor may at least force them to think about their prejudices. Parsia uses essentialism as a way to have fun: "You get people who are uncomfortable about [my marriage to a white man], and then I always decide to myself if I'm going to be amused by their discomfort and play it up or if I'll let them off the hook and make them more comfortable." Ursula, the white mother of three mixed-race children and one white child, told me about going shopping with her black partner: "We would go to Macy's or Stern's and go to the bedding department and try out the mattresses." She laughed. "Both of us would jump on the bed—and these salesmen would come flying up to us. We'd say, 'Oh, we were just trying out the mattresses.' Oh, we used to goof on them so bad. Sometimes people deserve it. I'm sorry, it's like, get over it, it's the 1990s." To use humor effectively, a multiracial family member must be well versed in the complexities of race and also be assured some level of safety. An interracial couple jumping on a bed together gives rise to threatening images of interracial sexuality. There are many situations that multiracial family members just choose to avoid.

### Conclusion

Unlike a Rorschach test, which involves a passive process of interpretation, multiracial family members actively name and claim racial identities. Judith Scales Trent, a black woman who appears white, writes about the effort Americans put into "doing" race, performing the racial script: "Stories about my life as a white black American also show that creating and maintaining a racial identity takes a lot of effort on my part, and on the part of other Americans. 'Race' is not something that just exists. It is a very demanding verb."[26] If race were inherent, something we were born with, then a genetic test would determine who belongs where. However race is constructed, contested, and shaped through the course of daily interaction, it is something we all actively do. The ways in which individuals think about race and their own racial identity influence their responses and interactions with others. In the 1950s and 1960s, the civil rights movement shifted how blacks thought about themselves. Today some hope that the multiracial movement will do the same for multiracial family members.

# 4

## *Communities,*

## *Politics, and*

## *Racial*

## *Thinking*

*Community* is the act or sense of sharing. Some communities are geographically defined, while others are not bound by physical location.[1] Some have a shared history and a common goal; others write their own histories as they form. Some are politically based; others share social, cultural, and historical experiences. We are assigned communities at birth; and we claim, disclaim, and build them throughout life. Inevitably, creating community means creating insiders and outsiders. Those on the inside fulfill some criteria. Those on the outside do not want to or cannot meet the criteria. These criteria are developed through negotiation both among community members and between the community and the larger society. In every case, negotiation involves battles about how to define, liberate, unite, exclude, and shape identities.

Historically, whites have defined racial communities as natural and inherent; individuals are assigned to these communities based on ancestral ties. Most people do not think about choosing and naming racial identities; historically, such a choice has even not been permitted.[2] Neil Gotanda says, "Generally speaking, these classifications are fixed; we cannot change our race to suit a personal preference. One does not arise in the morning and say, 'I think that today is my "white" day and tomorrow will be my "black" day.' "[3] Multiracial families, however, do not have either "white days" or "black days" and thus exemplify the mutability of racial communities. As they attempt to name their own experiences, communities, and identities, they confront powerful demands for racial conformity. At the same time, they learn that their own essentialist thinking can block their ability to name themselves and therefore create social justice.

Some members of multiracial families have begun referring to the *multiracial community*, and some have gone so far as to name the leadership.[4] Such a concept is fraught with problems. How far do community boundaries extend? Who is considered a member of this community? Only multiracial people? What about other multiracial family members? Will it include all mixes or just certain mixes? Will it include first-generation mixed-race people or all Americans who claim a mixed heritage? Where are the borders of this community, who will patrol them, and what are they protecting? Will a multiracial community lead to greater racial justice or greater societal divisions—one more layer in the racial hierarchy?

Despite obvious problems with defining *community*, an increasing number of organizations, web sites, magazines, and books as well as the common use of "our" when referring to multiracial families indicate that such communities may be forming.[5] But what is the basis of these

communities? At a minimum, all members of multiracial
families have faced some form of border patrolling that has
challenged them to question, shift, and claim varying identities at different times in their lives and in different situations. In fact, many family members see an escape from
border patrolling as the foundation for building multiracial
communities and networks. Cynthia Nakashima suggests
that multiracial people (and I extend her comments to most
members of multiracial families) share "certain themes and
issues" such as "locating one's racial/ethnic identity in various contexts and at different life stages, being pressured to
'choose' a monoracial identification by external forces, and
questions and issues of group belongingness and loyalty."[6]
According to these terms, then, such communities become
places for family members to avoid border patrollers as well
as explore racial identities. They give people opportunities
to relax and feel affirmed.

Unfortunately, when multiracial family members cite
border patrolling as their impetus for building community,
they lump black separatists with white supremacists; they
view black and white border patrollers as equally powerful.
By ignoring the white-supremacist system in which border
patrolling takes place, these families risk perpetuating
inequality in their search for comfortable social spaces. In
short, their primary concern becomes self-protection, not
social justice.

In my view, social justice must be a chief component in
the growth of multiracial communities. Until white
supremacy is undermined, the color line will remain intact,
and borderism will continue to be the primary method for
holding the line in place. The best way to dismantle white
supremacy is to firmly align ourselves with communities
struggling for liberation. The best way to reproduce white

supremacy is to struggle for color-blind policies that ultimately mask inequality under a facade of meritocracy.

In my research I have found that, as multiracial family
members struggle to create and find spaces where they can
feel comfortable and free from border patrolling, they often
lose sight of the larger racist system in which border patrolling
takes place. For example, in an attempt to "protect" multiracial family members, particularly children, from borderism, many are calling for a separate multiracial census
category. Some multiracial family members have even
evoked essentialist imagery and language in their claims that
multiracial people are biologically distinct from others.
Those searching for spaces of comfort and those advocating
for a separate multiracial category may unwittingly reproduce the color line and reinforce white supremacy. The
experiences of interracial couples who have adopted and
multiracial people who have been adopted highlight both the
essentialist shortcomings underlying contemporary debates
about transracial adoption and the pitfalls of color-blindness
in the adoption process. Their experiences help us understand
that "transracial adoption is a Band-Aid solution where far
more radical solutions are immediately needed."[7] Ultimately, attempts to use communities to avoid border
patrolling must begin with a concern for all oppressed people.
That is to say, when creating spaces of comfort, we must not
reproduce inequality and injustice.

### Informal Networks

"If you're invited to people's homes, you are either
with all white people or all black people; that's just the way
it is," lamented June. Given the ideological and objective
racial conditions in the United States, it is no surprise that

socializing in private homes and parties is generally done in same-race crowds. When people get together, they want to be able to relax and feel comfortable. Being with people of another race makes many Americans uncomfortable. Even when individuals are comfortable socializing across race lines, society provides few opportunities, outside of organized sports, the workplace, and perhaps nightclubs. For example, Joe, a white interracially married father, is uncomfortable socializing in single-race circles: "A lot of times we'll go to a Jewish wedding, and [my wife] will be the only black person at the wedding. And you're sort of disappointed because you'd like your friends to have as many black, white, and Asian friends as you do, but they just don't. . . . everybody stays with their own kind." Black and white co-workers, who may spend a great deal of time together at work, generally do not socialize outside of work-related events. Perhaps they like to stay close to home (unspoken text: neighborhoods are segregated) or prefer to spend leisure time with family (unspoken text: families are single race). Moreover, many blacks choose to be separated from whites during leisure time. After negotiating white-controlled institutions such as schools, work, and other business, many look forward to relaxing in settings where whites do not intrude. Some call this desired separation "black racism."[8] Unfortunately, by ignoring the larger white-supremacist context, this argument levels blacks and whites, holding each equally culpable for the segregation and thus the discrimination that multiracial family members face.

While many blacks choose social separation as a way to ameliorate the frustration caused by a white-controlled society, many multiracial family members choose diverse friendship networks as a way to avoid the effects of border patrolling. Because of single-race patterns of socializing, a multiracial family member is often "the only one" in a crowd unless she or he creates racially diverse situations. These situations may include interacting with other multiracial family members or bringing together people from many different backgrounds. In either scenario, these friendship circles are often consciously cultivated. Nancy, a thirty-year-old biracial woman living in Chicago, explained the difficult process she goes through to make sure her parties are mixed: "I try to sculpt my parties. The last one I had, there weren't many white people; and they all stood in the living room, and the black people stood in the kitchen, and I walked back and forth. It was frustrating. Let's face it: you go to a black party; alcohol is not all that important; the thing is to dance. At white parties they serve beer, and folks sit around talking. The balance is hard. I don't think most of my friends sit down and think about racially who they're going to invite. I do."

Echoing what I heard from so many others, Parsia explained why she and her husband make an effort to bring together people from different backgrounds: "When we go to parties at friends', it's usually single race. If we go to parties that blacks are throwing, it's all blacks; and if we go to parties that a white is throwing, it's all whites. One thing we noticed—when we have parties, it feels very different. We try to mix it up, which is really kind of cool. We always have a great time at our parties because neither [of us] is the only one of a certain race." In this way, Parsia and her husband create a space in which each feels comfortable.

Parties are specific events that can be planned and diversified through invitation lists. Long-term and close friendship networks do not work on the "RSVP by a certain date" system but develop or wither over time and through interaction. Rarely do most people entertain the idea of developing close friendships across race lines. For multiracial family members, such actions are conscious and deliberate. Friendship networks take many twists and turns based on how individuals identify racially at particular times in life. The desire to remove racists, border patrollers, and separatists from these networks reflects an attempt to avoid the frustration and turmoil caused by the color line.

For example, Daphne, who has light skin and racially ambiguous features, became militant as a teen and only wanted black friends. In this way, she was like many multiracial and transracially adopted people. Now a successful professional in her early thirties, she feels most comfortable around people who are racially mixed or open to others. She actively avoids militant people on either side: "I'm really happy in terms of the friendship choices that I've made in the past few years. I have started to steer myself away from having black friends or white friends who are militant. I am more comfortable with people who are more tolerant because otherwise it just creates too much turmoil all over again for me. I am most comfortable with people who are mixed because things get said in white groups and things get said in black groups, and it's hard for me within the context of my family." Likewise, Nancy reflected, "I no longer tolerate white friends who won't come to my parties. I don't have time for them anymore. I need people who feel comfortable in all different environments. My really close-knit group of friends are black, biracial, and Mexican and a white guy and one woman from Africa. At this point, if you can't be exploratory and open to all cultures, I don't have time to deal with you." By "mixing it up," multiracial family members reduce the strength of border patrolling in daily interactions. They are not necessarily challenging the color line, but they are ameliorating its effects. In short, they consciously "do" race while *choosing* friends so that they won't have to consciously "do" race while *with* their friends.

## Formal Organizations

Some people are unable to develop informal mixed friendship networks and thus turn to more formal organizations. Today there are more than six dozen formal multiracial family organizations across the United States. Some organizations are overtly political and work hard to challenge racial understandings that guide social policy. Others want to be social outlets and thus intentionally ignore larger racial politics. Most attempt to be both social and political. As the number of organizations indicates, many people are searching for a connection with other multiracial family members.

I have been involved in two of these organizations: Getting Interracial Families Together (GIFT), one chapter of which meets in Montclair, New Jersey; and the Biracial Family Network (BFN), which meets in downtown Chicago.[9] Each is struggling with a crucial community question: is it possible to create communities and spaces of comfort that do not exclude yet also challenge racism and social injustice? History has shown that multiracial family organizations can stay whole and strong by focusing on the shared experiences of border patrolling while avoiding larger racial politics. Indeed, this is the inherent flaw of multiracial family organizations: the very groups able to elucidate the dynamics of racism avoid these issues for fear of creating boundaries and exclusions and thus falling apart.

The Montclair chapter of GIFT was formed when a few interracially married women decided to do something for interracial families in Montclair after local teens harassed one family and vandalized their home. These women met with the original founders of GIFT in central New Jersey and decided that the organization's mission and name could be expanded to Montclair. This took some time because "the original founders wanted to make sure we would not, in any way, deal with political or religious issues. This was only to be a support network."[10] From its inception GIFT was to be a social outlet only.

By avoiding a political stance, some members think that GIFT will attract "all interracial and intercultural people and not exclude anyone."[11] They want GIFT to be a comfortable space in which multiracial family members will not have to deal with questioning looks and comments. These members fear that politics will create boundaries and exclusions, as it has in other communities. When opportunities arise that call for endorsement of a political position, GIFT as a organization remains neutral. This is interesting considering that the shared experiences of multiracial family members are directly linked to racism in society, which itself is highly political.

The original GIFT in central New Jersey nearly fell apart because of this social-only mission. Some members wanted it to be actively involved in antiracist causes, while the founders wanted it to remain strictly a social outlet. According to one founder, "just by being together in public, we are making a political statement." But what is this political statement? When the family is together, others interpret and analyze it according to their own political perspectives. At one end of the spectrum, multiracial families may indicate the impending assimilation of all groups. Thus, "just by being," they may provide strength for those who want to remove any mention of race from social policy and move quickly toward color-blind legislation. At the other end, white supremacists may see multiracial families as an indication of the decline of civilization. In this case, "just by being," these families tell the supremacists that they had better work harder. In short, calling "just by being" a political statement is no more than an attempt to remain neutral in a society in which race is anything but neutral. Remaining neutral will not shift the balance of racial power. Rather, those who remain neutral will, in effect, reproduce the status quo.

To this day, GIFT maintains a support-only mission and does not take official political stances. When blatantly political issues are brought to the fore, the organization distances itself. For instance, the following notice appeared in the March 1996 GIFT newsletter: "Charles Byrd, editor of Interracial Voice, is organizing a march on Washington, D.C. this coming July 20 in support of establishing a multiracial category on governmental forms. While GIFT is not taking a position on this issue as an organization, interested members are invited to contact Mr. Byrd."[12] Obviously, this issue is politically controversial and a major point of discussion among multiracial family members. Yet GIFT avoids taking a stance on anything that might lead to divisions.[13] Dorothy, a white interracially married mother and a member of GIFT, told me, "We have friends who we've brought in our group who are definitely not left wing, friends we have met just because they happen to be mixed-race couples and probably we would not have anything in common except for that." Unlike the civil rights movement, which needed to attend to life-threatening situations, GIFT and other multiracial organizations can choose not to be overtly political because multiracial families are not facing life-threatening persecution. Yet without an antiracism agenda, multiracial organizations seem to be distancing themselves socially and politically from blacks, creating one more layer in the racial hierarchy in which whites remain privileged, blacks disadvantaged, and multiracials somewhere in the middle.[14]

Nevertheless, such organizations are places where multiracial family members can catch a breath. Sheri, a twenty-three-year-old black and white woman living in Montclair, attended her first GIFT meeting in the mid-1990s: "When I went, it just felt really good, and everyone there is so friendly. It meant a lot to be there with everyone because they have either gone through or will go through the same things as me or can identify with me and understand—everyone! It makes me feel like I can express myself better." Likewise, Ursula, a white woman, treasures GIFT as a social outlet: "[Here] people are going through what I've been through over the years. I have black friends, and I have white friends. They are not in my shoes. They can listen, but they haven't been in that particular situation. But in a group like GIFT it's other people who are living or have lived what I live." Several people spoke about the comfort and safety they feel in a multiracial family group. June was involved in establishing the Montclair chapter: "I do see it growing, and I think it's great. People just want to know that there's a safe place to go. I think Montclair is about as good as it gets for raising biracial children, but it's still sometimes nice to just be in a group where you don't have to explain yourself, where people know right away who you are and what you deal with."

For parents, politics and concern for their children do not always mix. After a one GIFT meeting, Mina reflected, "This would have been a totally different discussion if it were a group of moms sitting around talking. It got pretty academic. The intellectual side is important, but we don't all have that language, although we do have the day-to-day, how-do-I-get-the-dishes-done experiences." Mina expresses the feeling of many multiracial family members, in particular parents. As Luis Rodriguez writes, "although the best way to deal with one's own children is to help construct the conditions that will ensure the free and healthy development of all, it's also true you can't be for all children if you can't be for your own."[15] With limited time together, families often prefer to focus on those things that will help them to negotiate borderism and raise healthy children: where to live, shop, and travel; find books, information, and multiracial-friendly professionals; track down a realtor, a lawyer, or an adoption agency. Nevertheless, focusing on these concerns alone does little to challenge the unjust color line.

In contrast, BFN, which was founded in 1980, does take overtly political stances as an organization. What started as a "parenting discussion and support group" has expanded.[16] In 1988, it "became a charter member of AMEA [the Association of MultiEthnic Americans]," thus taking a decidedly political turn.[17] AMEA was at forefront of lobbying congressional and other politicians for the addition of a multiracial category to the census and other governmental forms. In fact, Ramona Douglass, a multiracial woman and the current past president of AMEA and representative to the Census 2000 Advisory Board, is a past president of BFN. In a recent article, she lists BFN as one of the six "significant organizations across the nation" that have "set the tone and character of the interracial/multicultural movement."[18] Douglass writes for the *Interracial/Intercultural Connection*, the bimonthly newsletter of BFN. In the April 1996 issue she reaffirmed her goals for AMEA, with the support of organizations such as BFN: "My energy right now is focused on getting the multiracial category on the 2000 Census and increasing public awareness of the multiracial community's needs and experiences. . . . I'm learning a great deal about political influence and how the lack of it can stop even the most noble causes—I'm attempting to gain political clout for AMEA and our community in general."[19] BFN is politicized largely because it pays dues to AMEA each year. Even though individual members of multiracial families may be ambivalent about multiracial politics, by paying dues to BFN they are connected to the politically active umbrella organization. The general BFN membership (more than two hundred people) is not actively involved in multiracial politics. In fact, most members do not attend meetings on a regular basis but support BFN through dues because they like to know, as several people told me, that such an organization is in place "just in case."

Those who do attend meetings are primarily couples looking for a comfortable social outlet and parents who want help raising multiracial children. Quisha, a black interracially married expectant mother, told me: "Before I heard of BFN I was in a quandary about what to do about the kids. I didn't want them to deny their Irish heritage or their black heritage. Then I went to BFN, and I kept hearing 'biracial' and I thought, 'Yes! I've solved one issue.' Plus it's good to feel accepted. I think it's a basic human need."

But as these organizations solve some issues (at least for the moment), many more arise. If, for instance, being accepted is a need, then what will Quisha and others need to compromise to be accepted by other members of the organization? On some level she will not have to give up anything. She can attend the meetings, socialize with other multiracial families, talk about borderism, and then go back to her life until the next meeting. If the organization defines a clear political agenda, however, then she and others may be forced to define and defend their racial politics. As organizational boundaries become defined by racial politics rather than social experiences, individuals may feel alienated and less inclined to maintain membership. Such a concern led one former BFN president to conclude that "the organization needs to focus on the children, or it will fall apart." While BFN and other organizations avoid political issues, they have been the strength (perhaps unwittingly) behind the multiracial movement—those advocating for official recognition of multiracial people on the census and other governmental forms. Individuals search for comfortable social spaces, so they join BFN, the only multiracial family organization in Chicago.[20] BFN pays dues and supports AMEA. While individual members may be ambivalent about or not endorse the politics of those in the movement, their silence is read as tacit approval of AMEA's mission.

## Census Categories and the Construction of Race

As the U.S. Census Bureau tracks individuals according race, it creates race. Historically, local and federal agencies were not consistent in their definitions of racial groups. With the passing of civil rights legislation, however, the government needed to track and enforce compliance. In June 1974, a committee made up of representatives from various federal agencies was created to set forth broad definitions of racial and ethnic groups.[21] The committee "wanted to ensure that whatever categories the various agencies used could be aggregated, deaggregated and otherwise combined so that the data developed by one agency could be used in conjunction with another agency."[22] These categories would be used not just for the census but also for school forms, mortgage applications, employment forms, and loan applications as a way to monitor civil rights compliance and discrimination. By 1977, the Office of Management and Budget (OMB), the presidential office charged with overseeing the racial categories to be used on the census and other federal and local forms, had performed a monstrous feat: overseeing the creation of the broadly defined and consistent racial categories. The difficulty for OMB lay in the need to categorize people based on socially constructed inequalities and differences without essentializing race. To this end, OMB Directive No. 15, adopted on 12 May 1977, included the following caveat: "these classifications should not be interpreted as being scientific or anthropological in nature." Despite this note of caution, many continue to think about these categories as a reflection of essential race differences. The uniformity of racial categories made it possible to track the privileges received by individuals from one group and the discrimination faced by others. Yet at the same time, the color line was solidified.

The Census Bureau's designated racial categories left little room for complexities and differences.[23] The fourth question on the 1990 census form read, "Fill ONE circle for the race the person considers himself/herself to be." Individual family members could identify themselves as (1) black, (2) white, (3) American Indian or Alaska native, or (4) Asian or Pacific Islander. They could not claim more than one racial identity. If people did not want to fit themselves into one of the broad categories, they were forced fill in "other," the only remaining option. For these people the instructions specified, "If you fill in the 'other' race circle, be sure to print the name of the race," indicating that only one racial choice should be entered. If an individual chose to write in two or more races, the bureau considered only the first one listed, which became the category under which the person was were tabulated. For instance, a multiracial individual who wrote "white, black, and Native American" was tabulated as "white." People who wrote "black and white" were tabulated as "black."[24]

After the 1990 census, OMB organized a national discussion about the possibility of changing racial categories for Census 2000. As decisions were made about racial categories, debates raged in the press, the academy, civil rights organizations, and the government about the possible addition of a multiracial category. Local and national newspapers ran articles and op-eds on a regular basis. Multiracialism became front-page news. Congress held hearings; OMB conducted test questionnaires and held public meetings. Maria P. P. Root's 1996 edited collection *The Multiracial Experience* was given to all the members of OMB's Race and Ethnicity Advisory Committee so they could "better familiarize themselves with socio-political ideologies/identity issues facing multiracials today."[25] Some multiracial family members and organizations actively lobbied for the category. Sometimes dubbed the multiracial movement, the group became involved in letter campaigns, public speaking, and activism within multiracial family organizations. In July 1996 it organized a rally and march in Washington, D.C.[26]

Nevertheless, after many meetings, test forms, public discussions, and contact with researchers around the country, OMB decided that Census 2000 should maintain the traditional racial categories, with an added option of "check one or more boxes." This option means that tabulation of racial categories will include sixty or so possibilities. Those charged with tabulating the categories, including researchers, civil rights enforcers, and the Census Bureau, are unhappy with this decision, as are some members of the multiracial movement. Jane Ayers Chiong laments that the decision "still leaves multiracial students without a specific identity when answering, 'What race are you?' on school forms."[27] She points out that the decision keeps the monoracial system of counting in place. Others, however, such as Ramona Douglass, see the decision as a break with "the rigidity with which we as a nation have held racial boundaries."[28] She is now concentrating her efforts on ensuring that the new tabulation method will not harm civil rights protections. But others in the multiracial movement are becoming more vocal in their demands that multiracial people be recognized as a unique racial group, particularly those promoting *multiracial* as a new race or as the means for dismantling the color line and white supremacy.

## The Politics of Multiracialism and Census Categories

Arguments for the inclusion of a multiracial category tend to fall into two broad groups. Each draws on the liberal tenets of individual rights over group rights by suggesting that multiracial people should have the right to identify themselves. One group, however, argues that multiracial people constitute a new race and refer to biological differences between multiracial people and others.[29] The other group suggests that a multiracial category will ultimately undermine the color line by working against the myth of white racial purity and the one-drop rule. In short, the first group argues that race is essential and objective; adding a multiracial category is a way to be more accurate.[30] The second group suggests that race, while historically constructed, is merely an illusion; adding a multiracial category will explode the illusion. In fact, both of these arguments fall short. Race is neither illusionary nor essential. It is a social construction that has created objective conditions of injustice. Any struggle to restructure racial categories should, at a minimum, address social justice; and this may be possible only by articulating private and public racial identities.[31]

Essentialist Arguments. Essentialist arguments make two assumptions: (1) race is a biological phenomenon; and (2) racial identities, like race, are determined by DNA and are thus immutable. As Charles Byrd said during the 1996 multiracial march on Washington, D.C., "no principled multiracial can endorse separate but equal. How can we? We are the living, breathing antithesis of separatist and racist dogma. We cannot be separated!"[32] Many people want a multiracial category because they believe multiracial children are threatened if they are not "accurately" racially classified. For instance, when baseball player Rod Carew's mixed-race daughter needed a bone marrow transplant, multiracial family organizations were targeted for bone marrow donations.[33] These organizations put up little opposition to such targeting; in fact, many used the family's crisis as a reason to increase demands for an officially recognized category. Pushing the idea of bone marrow collection at the 1996 march, Ramona Douglass, then president of AMEA, stated, "We are doing this today in loving memory of Karen Raez[,] one of our multiracial children who died of leukemia after an unsuccessful donor search."[34]

Biological arguments extend beyond bone marrow. Project RACE, created in 1991 to fight for the inclusion of a multiracial category on governmental forms, posted an "urgent medical concern" notice on its web site. The heading "They Should Know Better!" is followed by a complaint about the National Committee on Vital and Health Statistics, which agreed with OMB's 1997 decision to "NOT include the use of the term Multiracial." The statement reads: "This committee should recognize that the proposed tabulation of racial data is *not good*. The revised OMB directive may not provide *any* information on health for the multiracial population. The National Committee on Vital and Health Statistics should be working toward 'truth in racial and ethnic tabulation' instead of accepting the discriminatory practices of this administration."[35] Such an argument assumes that first-generation biracial people who have one black and one white parent are genetically distinct from the estimated 80 percent of African Americans who have multiracial ancestry and the unknown percentage of whites who are unaware of or hide their multiracial ancestry.[36] It takes for granted that people who identify as black share a common genetic makeup, as do people who identify as white, and that blacks and whites are genetically distinct. Based on such logic, black-white multiracial people are also biologically distinct.[37] Yet there is greater genetic variation among whites and among blacks than between blacks and whites.

In *From Black to Biracial,* Kathy Odell Korgen argues for the addition of a multiracial category by pointing out the need to have a separate multiracial drug testing group:

> One pharmaceutical company created a drug to fight hypertension. They recommended that white persons take one milligram and black persons consume two milligrams per dosage. When questioned what size dosage multiracial persons should consume, the company admitted they had no idea. No multiracial persons were included in the clinical trials of the drug, emphasizing the fact that recognition of such a category is important not only for the psychological and social well-being of this population, but also for their physical health.[38]

Trying to move one step forward, Korgen tripped and fell two steps backward by assuming that people who claim a multiracial identity are biologically different from those who claim a single-race black identity or single-race white identity. Beyond this, her biologically based arguments do not attend to the larger multiracial population: people of various mixes beyond black and white. Wouldn't defining a broad multiracial category actually move researchers further away from being able to run more accurate clinical trials (or the census, for that matter)? Would a person who is Asian and black be grouped with someone who is Native American, white, and Asian? Each is multiracial, but why should the two be grouped together for purposes of bone marrow or clinical trials? Is a person with one Japanese parent and one Chinese parent mixed? What about someone who is Greek and Irish? When census categories are sliced one way, they create major differences among those assigned to different racial groups. When sliced another way, they mute differences among members assigned to the same racial group.

Biologically based arguments will do little bring about social justice, and they certainly will not help to create more sophisticated racial understandings. Instead, they rehash simplistic understandings of race that historically have been used to maintain white supremacy. A multiracial category and an officially recognized community would create greater divisions, and society would not necessarily be pushed to think more critically about race and racial identities. Whites could just recategorize this group of racially mixed people and, with calm certainty, once again see themselves as superior.

"The Category Will Explode Myths" Argument. Some argue that officially recognizing and defining a multiracial community through a census category will call into question the boundaries of blackness and whiteness and undermine the myth that race is biologically clear-cut. They see a multiracial category as a way to undermine the myth of white racial purity and the one-drop rule, which are grounded in the idea of race as a biological phenomenon. Byrd says, "Contemporary advocacy of a mixed-race identifier is the largest and most meaningful assault on the concept of white racial purity/supremacy . . . to come down the pike in many moons."[39] He points out that, although whites created the myth, leaders of color have embraced the one-drop rule and are thus also responsible for reproducing the myth. A multiracial category would be flooded, he suggests, thus revealing the myths on which the racist system has been structured.

Another variation of this argument is that, because the one-drop rule stigmatizes blacks, a multiracial category will end such stigmatization by removing the rule's underpinnings. Julie Lythcott-Haims argues that when parents raise multiracial children as black, they "perpetuate the notion that Blackness is a stigma. . . . they implicitly adopt the 'one-drop' approach, which demeans persons of African and part-African ancestry since it treats 'Black blood' differently than any other blood by stigmatizing it as a contaminant. Referring to these children only as 'Black,' thereby denying the rest of their cultural ancestry, adopts the racist classification scheme devised by White shareholders for the purpose of perpetuating the slave trade."[40]

The myth of white racial purity, based on a biological notion of race, is indeed the foundation upon which the U.S. racist system was constructed. Yet a multiracial category will not challenge purity as the basis for whiteness. As Nancy, a biracial attorney from Chicago, told me, "In general, I have found that as long as you don't say you're white, whites don't care what you call yourself; they have no problem with the multiracial category." Naming another category does not detract from white privilege; it may simply help individual whites fine-tune identities grounded in notions of superiority.

A struggle for individual and social justice must include a politic that recognizes how socially constructed injustices have become embedded in American institutions. Those struggling for justice must address institutional inequalities by engaging in practices that will undermine the essentialist and racist thinking that drives borderism. Otherwise, they may be complicit with a system of white supremacy. Lisa Jones asks, "Instead of fighting for a new racial category, if the end goal is, as census activists say, to do away with the biological psuedoscience of race, why aren't they in the trenches casting stones at institutional racism?"[41] The privileges granted to whites in a white-supremacist society cannot be undermined by a multiracial classification. In fact, as whites lose their demographic majority, they may encourage greater divisions within communities of color.[42] Addressing institutional racism and borderism simultaneously may require individuals to identify themselves publicly in one way, privately in another.

### Political Choices about Representing Ourselves

In an interview on National Public Radio Lise Funderburg spoke of "claiming public and private identities" as a method for negotiating within a society that demands conformity to a single racial group identification.[43] While racial categories are imposed and maintained through borderism, our identities are fluid and can be claimed according to our politics. Racial categories are imposed in that all white people receive some privileges because they are seen as white and all black people face racist abuse because they are seen as black. (In each case, privilege and abuse are moderated by gender, sexual orientation, class, and so on.) Yet imposed racial categories based on essentialist racial myths include many communities with very different agendas: nationalist, socialist, conservative, liberal, separatist, pluralist, integrationist, Christian, Jew, Muslim, orthodox, reform, gay, lesbian, and more.

We have an obligation to align ourselves with communities concerned about the liberation of all oppressed people. Many black-white multiracial family members who oppose the formation of a multiracial community and category have specific political motivations. They may believe, for instance, that such a category will undermine the already shrinking protections in place for African Americans. These people may claim a different, more complex racial identity on an individual level but claim black as a public identity.[44] Daphne noted: "I have always identified myself as black, although if people ask me specifically, "do I have any white in me?" I will answer honestly. It's not a big deal, but I identify with issues minorities are faced with much easier than I do with a typical white person." Dorothy, a white interracially married mother of two who no longer defines herself as white, agreed that important reasons exist for multiracial families to align themselves with the African Americans: "Mariah is only three, and she doesn't understand yet that color makes a difference, but I put her down as black. I would prefer her to be representing a black group because there is just too much power in the hands of whites."

In *The New Colored People: The Mixed-Race Movement in America*, Jon Michael Spencer calls on multiracial people with African ancestry to align with black communities. At the same time, he points out that African Americans "must open up new space for mixed-race blacks to be biracially black. . . . African Americans must not place membership restrictions on mixed-race people who say they are half black. . . . the black community cannot hold certain of its members in limbo, feeling uneasy about interracial marriages or their biracialness, and expect them to wait for acceptance."[45] Citing Itabari Njeri, he suggests that if blacks do not open their borders, "they are simply forcing the creation of a multiracial classification by forcing the exodus of mixed-race blacks from even a partial black identity."[46] The need for solidarity against white supremacy requires the recognition that the color line is not static and borders are not fixed and unchanging. Likewise, multiracial family members, like Daphne and Dorothy, must begin to acknowledge, discuss, and act on the connection between borderism and white supremacy. That is, black communities have used border patrolling as protection against white supremacy. If white supremacy did not exist, then black border patrolling of black-white multiracial family members would diminish.

Unfortunately, multiracial people often cite black border patrolling as an impetus in the struggle for a multiracial category without acknowledging white supremacy. For instance, Charles Byrd says, "Afrocentric Nationalism by the black community coupled with the 1967 Supreme Court decision overthrowing the remaining anti-miscegenation laws in this country are the two most important factors in the genesis of the multiracial movement."[47] But Gary Peller notes, "To be sure, much nationalist rhetoric was reductionist with respect to the complexity of group relations . . . but through the identification of racial identity and group-consciousness as central to the structure of American social relations, the black nationalists of the sixties also identified the particular aspect of black liberation assumed—the commitment by whites to deny the centrality of race as a historically constructed, powerful factor in the social structure of American life."[48] Thus, as blacks struggle for liberation and multiracial family members struggle for recognition, each blames the other for the lack of acceptance. On the one hand, Byrd notes, "I submit that it is *not* the mixed-race movement that is 'distancing' itself from 'color' but quite the reverse."[49] On the other, Lisa Jones blames multiracials when she points out that in the struggle for a multiracial census category there existed no alliances between multiracials and progressive organizations of color: "None of these [multiracial] organizations had staged a teach-in or protested over the miscarriage of justice in the Rodney King case."[50]

It is one thing to seek comfortable spaces that give us a sense of belonging; it is another to demand that a particular identity be officially recognized. Some people hope that claims to a multiracial identity will dilute racial categories into nonexistence—and perhaps they will, given the browning of America.[51] The category could even become a unifier against a system of whiteness. Nevertheless, a state-legitimized multiracial classification may also blur clear signs of whiteness.[52] Multiracial family members are at a crossroads and must decide how to proceed. As we do, we must recognize and address race as a system of power. We must balance our desire to create spaces of comfort with the struggle for social justice and the liberation of all communities of color.

## Who's an Us and
## Who's a Them? Debating Adoption

Issues of community, identity, and politics weave through debates about transracial adoption. Transracial adoption debates and struggles are almost always about white parents gaining access to children of color, not parents of color gaining access to white children.[53] Until the recent explosion of intercountry adoptions, questions regarding transracial adoption were debated almost exclusively between white couples trying to adopt black children and the National Association of Black Social Workers (NABSW), which was attempting to place black children with black parents. Given the fact that the majority of transracial adoptions are made up of "children who are not either black or white," the fiery debate between white parents and black social workers highlights the threat posed to communities and identities when the color line is crossed.

Today, interracially married people and adults who were transracially adopted as children are also entering the debate, and they may raise many more questions about racial understandings and injustice. If a white mother puts her multiracial baby up for adoption, who is best suited to raise that child? A black family? A multiracial family? All else being equal, what makes one family more qualified than the other? What role should skin color play in the process of placement? Who should make these decisions? This is exactly what Daphne refers to when she asks, "Who's making these category decisions? That's the killer. It's typically one side or the other, black versus white, as opposed to someone who has all those experiences. We need to find more mixed-race adopted people and get some input."

When I began my research, I wanted to hear about the experiences of transracial adoption from adults who had lived it. I soon discovered another unheard population: interracial couples who have adopted. The experiences of these parents reveal an essentialist system that closely ties race to notions of skin color and uses skin color as the litmus test for matching. In such a system blacks are devalued, whites valued, and multiracial children assigned an in-between status.[54]

Transracial adoption has been publicly debated since 1972, when NABSW gained enough political strength to speak out against a white-controlled child welfare system. Immediately the number of black children placed in white families dropped dramatically. Couched in larger debates of individual versus group rights and nationalism versus integrationism, transracial adoption has been hotly debated by people who consider themselves to be either white or black. On one side are color-blind policy advocates who argue that we should ignore race when placing a child with a family. Drawing on western tenets of individual rights, they suggest that the U.S. courts' "best interest of the child" criteria should be the foremost concern. They argue that by considering race in the adoption process, black children and other children of color are needlessly raised in institutional care rather than in loving families. On the other side of the debate are race-matching policy advocates who argue that because historically grounded racial inequalities are still pervasive, placing a black child with a white family is, at the extreme, a form of cultural genocide.[55] Drawing on group-rights criteria, they suggest that the best interests of a child are only addressed when the grievances of the oppressed group to which that child belongs are addressed.

### Color-Blind Policy Advocates

Color-blind policy advocates argue that we need to remove race from adoption decisions because it offends the traditional, legal, and philosophical underpinnings of the humanist ideal of equality central to the Constitution. They reduce the issue to two questions: (1) how do adoption policies fit with the prevailing ideologies of the United States? and (2) what is in the best interest of each individual child awaiting placement? As Peter Hayes asserts, "African American separatists [oppose the] humanist philosophy of the Civil Rights Movement." He claims that "minority children placed for adoption have neither the right nor the need to develop a distinct ethnic identity or awareness of cultural heritage."[56] Such liberal humanists believe that socially created differences and inequalities should be ignored and all people treated the same.[57] As a result, many color-blind advocates conclude that race-based policies (and politics) are responsible for perpetuating racial significance in society and thus dividing the human community.[58] Since we are all the same, they suggest, individual rights should be privileged over group rights. For instance, Harvard law professor Randall Kennedy argues that "race matching reinforces racialism. It strengthens the baleful notion that race is destiny. It buttresses the notion that people of different racial backgrounds really are different in some moral, unbridgeable, permanent sense. It affirms the notion that race should be a cage to which people are assigned at birth and from which people should not be allowed to wander."[59] Nevertheless, he fails to note that race *is* a cage to which people are assigned at birth. Perhaps the clearest indicator of this cage, of the centrality of race and racism, are the race-related price tags placed on children available for adoption. Race as skin color is the primary basis for pricing. As evidence, in 1990 a U.S. agency published a price list for adoption: white children cost $7,500, biracial children $3,800, and black children $2,200.[60] These price tags are clues to the larger social inequities lying behind the adoption issue.

Those suggesting that any discussion of race or special treatment programs simply continues racialism tend to talk *only* about how society is racialized rather than the interplay between racialization and racism. For example, Yehudi O. Webster suggests that once we recognize racial categories, people join sides and "in the resulting racial dogfights, citizens become hypersensitized about anatomical differences and cannot see the human forest for the racial trees. . . . this condition of enforced racial awareness is then referred to as a social reality and a justification for further racial research and policies on race."[61] Rather than acknowledging racism and white supremacy as reasons why we need research and social policies, he suggests that the research and social policies themselves set the stage for "racial dog fights."

These theorists all overlook the history of subjugation and oppression faced by many groups of color in an unjust racist system. Suggesting that race matching racializes without acknowledging the significance of race in all our lives takes transracial adoption out of its social context. Neil Gotanda suggests that "a color-blind interpretation of the Constitution legitimates and thereby maintains the social, economic, and political advantages that whites hold over other Americans."[62] Instead of addressing the historical creation of race and racial communities, color-blind advocates often cite statistics and "facts" about the large number of black children pouring into the child welfare system. They then conclude that transracial adoption should be encouraged. For instance, Simon et al.'s *The Case for Transracial*

*Adoption* argues that "in contrast to the evidence on which the case *for* transracial adoption rests, the case *against* transracial adoptions is built primarily on ideology and rhetoric."[63] Rather than examining the historic and contemporary racial conditions in the United States, for which empirical data exist, the authors explain that black children are the victims of a discriminatory system that will not place them transracially "in a society committed to racial colorblindness."[64]

Is our society really committed to racial color-blindness, or is this just rhetoric? Should we be committed to color-blindness, or is this a misguided goal? In other words, does racial color-blindness equal racial justice? The answer is, of course, no. In fact, racial color-blindness protects institutionalized racial inequalities. Quickly overlooked by most who argue in favor of color-blind transracial adoption is a discussion of *why* so many children of color are in the care of the child welfare system. The importance of racism and the need for racial unity are ignored in the struggle to define all humans as essentially the same.

### Race-Matching Advocates

Race-matching advocates suggest that since race is central to all our lives and threatens oppressed people, we should acknowledge it and build communities of solidarity to fight for liberation. In other words, ignoring the centrality of race in society will lead to inappropriate policies and exacerbate the disadvantages blacks face in a white-supremacist system.[65] Advocates for race-matching policies ask, "What about the best interest of *all* children, particularly black children, given the continued oppression and racism in society?" They claim a community boundary with an underlying premise that individuals defined as black share a universal experience with white supremacy. Moreover, they imply that authenticism can, on some level, be determined and achieved: that "our" children and "your" children can be differentiated.

As we have discussed, this form of essentialism has historically allowed blacks to unite and fight for liberation. To some extent, however, racial matching argues that race can be located within the individual. For instance, a 1986 NASBW position paper argued, "Black children belong, physically, psychologically and culturally in Black families in order that they receive the total sense of themselves and develop a sound projection of their future. . . . Black children in white homes are cut off from the healthy development of themselves as Black people. . . .We the participants of the workshop have committed ourselves to go back to our communities and work to end this particular form of genocide."[66] A 1994 NABSW position paper begins by quoting the *Journal of Law and Family:* "In a society where race is socially identified and socially emphasized, one must seriously question whether the best interests of a black child may be distinguished from the child's inherent race."[67] Clearly, as Kennedy suggests, such a position reinforces the strength of the essentialist color line. Nevertheless, given the continued centrality of race and racism in society, blacks do need to protect community boundaries and rally on behalf of black children. Removing race from placement decisions does not address *why* so many children of color are moving into the child welfare system.

Both race-matching and color-blind policy advocates believe that clearly defined communities of sameness are possible and worth fighting for. As contrary as these camps appear to be, they share ideals of universalism and essentialism: color-blind advocates do not recognize the importance of race in society, ignoring social differences while making claims for an essential human experience. Advocates for race-matching subsume many differences under the umbrella of blackness.[68] Not generally considered are inter-racially married adoptive parents and multiracial adopted children (whom transracial adoption studies typically refer to as black).[69] When their experiences are examined, it becomes more difficult to take one side or the other. Most interracially married adoptive couples and most adopted multiracial children advocate strongly for transracial adoption, although not in a color-blind manner.

## Interracial Couples and Adoption

In the mid-1990s I joined an adoption reading group at the City University of New York because I assumed that interracial couples would have the greatest difficulty adopting and wanted to learn as much as possible about the process. Many people, particularly whites, had told me they were concerned about the treatment any offspring of interracial relationships would receive in a racially divided world, and I presumed this concern would extend to adoption agencies.[70] The first article we read, Elizabeth Bartholet's "Where Do Black Children Belong? The Politics of Race Matching in Adoption," affirmed my suspicions.[71] In a footnote, she noted that "an interracial couple (white husband, black wife) that recently applied to a D.C. adoption agency was told by the agency that they would be placed very low on the priority list for a mixed-race child. The first preference was to assign such a child to a couple who were both mixed race, with darker skinned Black couples next in line, and Black singles third."[72]

Then I began talking with interracial couples who had adopted. It seems that the agency Bartholet referred to is an anomaly. In fact, if the birth mothers of multiracial children choose to place their children with an interracial couple, the agencies involved struggle to locate such couples. Generally, when interracial couples express interest in either fostering or adoption, the child welfare system responds positively and fast. According to my research, interracial couples are in high demand for both fostering and adopting children, particularly multiracial ones. The couples with whom I spoke were each given a child quickly (in nine months or less), were placed on a preferred adoption list, and were asked repeatedly to adopt more children. Joe, a white interracially married father living in a wealthy, predominantly white neighborhood, thought that he and his wife were able to adopt quickly and easily because "most people want to adopt a white child. We didn't want a white child. We wanted a mixed race or black child. I think once we were licensed, they had a child for us in two weeks. Most people wait a year. Our lawyer presented us with the possibility that we might have to choose and that was tough because nobody ever has to choose, but ten days later we had two children to choose from."

Likewise, Barbara, who lives in a black suburb of Chicago, told me, "I was expecting an eight-year wait for a healthy child; I only waited nine months for my son. After we adopted him, they called and asked if we wanted a girl. It was really incredible. See, they are considered special-needs children, which is bizarre, because they are perfectly healthy babies. And then it is interesting, but we, as an interracial couple, are considered a resource." Ingrid, a white interracially married mother living in a predominantly white, working-class community on Long Island, shared a similar experience: "We were surprised how quickly it happened. It was just three and a half months, and we had our daughter. We were not prepared because it happened so fast and we were told that the birth mother just wouldn't look at another couple; she wanted a biracial couple. They always ask the birth mother to choose a backup in case, and she refused; she only wanted us."

Whether living in a wealthy, poor, or working-class area; a predominantly black or white area, interracial couples are generally able to adopt mixed-race children quickly and easily. Several factors intersect to make the placement of mixed-race children with interracial couples quicker than most people expect. First, for couples involved in open adoptions, the birth mother can choose who will adopt her child. In each case just discussed, the birth mother demanded that an interracial couple adopt the child. Next, agencies that maintain closed adoptions often attempt to "pass" the family as a biologically connected group and thus search for interracial couples to parent multiracial children. The assumption is that a multiracial baby with an interracial couple will appear natural. This in itself creates a unique set of problems because naturalness is often judged by skin color.

Agencies have been known to attempt to match skin color—assuming, apparently, that they can tell what the child of an interracial couple's skin color should be. For example, Ingrid and her husband adopted a multiracial daughter. Ingrid's husband is a very light-skinned black man who is often mistaken for white. When they decided to adopt, they faced few problems until the day they were supposed to pick up their new daughter: "The agency called, 'Congrats, you're the parents of a baby girl.' Then they called back, 'Wait a minute; the baby might be too dark for you. She is brown, and that's not what we had in mind for you. We wanted tan.' That's what they said! It was like shopping for a pair of shoes or something. If we had a baby biologically, we wouldn't know what color it would be. So what's the problem?" After several phone conversations and a great deal of frustration, Ingrid and her husband decided to drive to upstate New York and pick up their newborn daughter anyway. They finally persuaded the agency to agree with them. Nearly nine years later, these memories are still vivid for Ingrid. The idea of matching skin tones shows a misunderstanding about the broad variation of physical features within individual families. Within black, Latino, and multiracial families, children can vary widely in appearance. It is common for babies to darken in their first few months, and hair texture is never a given at birth.

As an attorney, Nancy, a biracial woman, has worked with many interracial couples who would like to adopt. She told me that "most mixed couples definitely want a mixed baby. I mean, when you think about it, you would expect more out of a mixed-race couple, but they are doing the same thing as all these black parents who say they want a black baby and all these white parents who want a white baby. They all want the baby to look like themselves. So if it's a mixed-race couple, they want a mixed-race kid so the kid looks like they were a product of their union." Clearly, Nancy believes that multiracial family members should have a more sophisticated understanding of race because they have been given many opportunities to think about it. Yet because these opportunities often relate to borderism, couples may be attempting to avoid further intrusions. Contrary to Nancy's observation, I noted that people didn't have a preference for mixed over black, but each ultimately adopted a mixed-race baby (or babies) because of pushes from agencies and birth mothers.

The common denominator that each couple shared was not requesting a white baby. Parsia and her husband were presented with the option of adopting a Russian baby and ultimately decided against it because of the power issues race would present if Parsia and her baby were in public together. "We could have done a Russian adoption easily and quickly, but whether or not I could be real comfortable rearing a white child was another question. I really thought I would not be comfortable. It would be weird. I had the thought that everyone would think I was the nanny or servant, no one would think I'm this child's mother, and the whole thought that a cop could challenge you about being this child's mother. And always having to explain—that, I thought would be very difficult." The politics of race and the historical imbalance of power loomed large in her decision. While not embraced by society, a white mother with children of color does not shift the balance of power from parent to child. But when the parent is black and the child appears white, the black parent is undermined as white society attempts to keep its privileges by maintaining the "proper order of things."

### Multiracial People and
### Adoption: Race Matters, Love Matters

Each adopted individual with whom I spoke advocated for the removal of formal and informal race barriers in adoption, albeit with reservations.[73] The empirical research carried out to date overwhelmingly supports making transracial adoption a viable alternative to institutionalization. A recent and rare study about multiracial children and adoption revealed that multiracial children were being mistreated in a system governed by institutional and individual borderism. In 1993, Gail Folaron and Peg McCartt reported on their two-year study of mixed-race children in the child welfare system in Indiana. They found that the system attempted to walk a line between race matching and color-blind practices and in doing so failed to address adequately the "unique needs of children of mixed racial parentage." The Children and Family Services manual of Indiana states that "biracial and multiracial children would be most appropriately reared by an adoptive family of the minority race or in a family in which at least one of the parents is of the child's minority race."[74] Yet agencies did not address race when they placed multiracial children in foster care or adoption: "the informal agency placement policy . . . for children of mixed African American and Caucasian parentage was with African American foster parents, but in practice, these homes were generally reserved for African American children."[75] With black homes reserved for darker-skinned African American children as well as a lack of interracial couples, black-white multiracial children were sent to white homes, and workers then chose to ignore race completely. "In the foster parents' experience, caseworkers and service providers tended to deny or ignore the significance of the children's racial identity."[76] When the significance of race was ignored, so was the opportunity to educate adoptive or foster parents about race.

Each multiracial adoptee with whom I spoke advocated strongly that children should be placed with a loving family rather than languish in institutional care. Each added, however, that children should not be placed in a color-blind manner. For instance, Lauren, a forty-two-year-old multiethnic woman with light skin, sandy-brown hair, and green eyes, was adopted by white parents when she was twelve years old. Before then she lived in orphanages and was bounced in and out of foster homes. She was never told about her racial background until a social worker heard her and some other children chanting, "Nigger, nigger, nigger," at a passerby. Lauren remembered, "By the time I was nine, I'd already been in ten foster homes, and I was in an orphanage for the second time. There was a social worker outside at the orphanage, and she stopped us and called me over to her and asked me why I was doing that because didn't I know I was a nigger too. That was my introduction to my ethnicity. I was devastated. I had never heard anything good about anybody black, and it was very hard to deal with." Now equipped with an understanding of why she was not adopted or placed permanently with a family at an earlier age, Lauren lamented, "All things being equal, then, you make the [race-matching] placement, but you don't do what they did to me. They kept bouncing me around thinking that they would hit on the right combination, but it didn't work. You don't bounce kids around waiting for the right thing or until they are old enough so it won't be an issue. You don't do that to children. Maybe I wouldn't have had to be a nine-year-old totally aghast that I was a nigger. It didn't have to be that way, I could have learned at two when I first became available for adoption, and I could have learned that in more positive terms." Lauren would like to see some form of screening and programs that help parents who adopt across race lines to know how to present life in more positive terms. Eventually she was adopted by white parents who moved to a black neighborhood and were very active in the civil rights movement. Lauren learned to be proud of being black through the many experiences provided by her family and their friends.

Each individual with whom I spoke suggested that his or her particular adoption worked (or could have worked better) because families did not ignore race but addressed race issues regularly. Marguerite told me, "My mother and this other [black] woman I started getting close to talked all the time. My parents encouraged it; they knew I needed that. They knew I needed to identify myself, and they would get up in the morning and drive me to black church and come back and get me. It was totally encouraged. As I look back now, I can see what my mother was doing. Then I was just a selfish teenager, and I didn't think much of it. I'm sure she knew I was curious, so she wanted me to be exposed to all of this." The ability of white adoptive parents to provide access to African American cultural identity and role models was a central concern of many adoptees.

Marguerite's parents also made discussions of racism a

part of daily life: "When we went to buy a new home it was an open conversation about having us with them and the way certain people might react, and there was very open conversation about our neighbors being prejudiced if they saw that. If my mom and dad were having a conversation, it wasn't hidden from us. . . . My parents were real good about getting black dolls and bringing us to the DuSable Museum, and that was back when getting black dolls was not that easy. And nothing, nothing was ever secret."

Lauren spoke about the importance of her parents' networks and their openness about racial issues: "My parents had a very diverse group of friends, ethnically, economically. . . . There were things I didn't know, like why it would be good to be a black person. All I ever saw was that if you were a black person, people didn't like you, and my folks thought it very important that I understand what's good about it. I was lucky because my parents were very involved in the civil rights movement. We had people in our house. When they came to town to speak, my parents always put them up—so, for example, the man who got me to stop biting my fingernails was Stokely Carmichael." She also credits her parents for leaving their all-white neighborhood and moving to a predominantly black area that was a hotbed of civil rights and black power activity: "I had all these strong black people around me, so learning about being a black person and feeling good about being a black person was just incredible for me, and I really credit my parents. When they decided to adopt me, they decided to move out of a predominantly white neighborhood and move into a more ethnically diverse area." Thus, as Lauren and others suggest and empirical research verifies, transracial adoptions do work as long as adoptive parents work to understand how race is constructed in society and how they themselves construct race through the adoption.[77]

Although interracial couples, especially black and white couples, are often seen as social pariahs, they are a resource in the world of adoption. This priority status is granted in large part because of attempts to match children to parents based on skin color. Multiracial and black children are portrayed as special-needs cases, and those willing to adopt such children are often painted as heroes. White children, in contrast, are viewed as angels (reflected in their higher price tag) and those adopting them as blessed. When a white couple adopts a black child, others assume they are good liberals who are making a sacrifice. The social conditions that create large numbers of parentless children of color, both in the United States and abroad, have yet to be seriously addressed. These conditions include economic inequality, racism, lack of affordable housing, lack of opportunity, and patriarchy.

As government spending is cut and the poor, especially poor blacks, find themselves more disenfranchised, more children will need homes. Thus, removing race-conscious politics in adoption is merely a Band-Aid for a larger problem based at the intersection of race and class inequality. Yet children currently in the system deserve loving homes regardless of race. All children, today and in the future, deserve a world that values and acts on the ideals of equality and justice.

## Conclusion

Perhaps nothing has brought multiracial families into conversations about the formation of community and new identities more than the census debate. The possibility that the official naming of racial categories could change social dynamics has compelled many to think about the issues at stake: identity, racial justice, self-esteem, and social comfort, among others. Some time ago I received an e-mail message about the Census 2000 committee hearings that was sent to interested parties and researchers. The sender, a well-known advocate for a multiracial category, was happily announcing Newt Gingrich's support for the category. I responded with a lengthy admonishment about the problem of building community around multiracialism without a keen eye to larger politics:

> Have you asked yourself why Mr. Gingrich is backing a multiracial category and promoting the idea of a multiracial community? He is also promoting color-blind legislation. The two are connected. Have you looked at the demographics of the Senate and the House lately? What about the CEOs of top companies? With power firmly in the hands of these white men, it is in their interest to call political agendas that will encourage color-blind platforms. They want to stop talking about race and pretend it doesn't exist so that they can claim that we have a level playing field. They'd like to argue that they merit their positions of power and privilege. As members of multiracial families, we need to be very careful about whom we align ourselves with politically. There is a larger racial and political struggle going on. Are we going to align ourselves with people who fight for the liberation of all human beings, or are we fighting for a cause that may ultimately worsen the life chances of a large number of African Americans and others? I am not opposed to the struggle for the right to self-identify as long as it is in the context of a critical and politically astute movement.

Within a day the sender informed me, "This is a battle about power (*the* multiracial community against single-race communities) and we need support from whomever we can get it."

Less antagonistically, multiracial family members often

say that they perceive themselves as a bridge between blacks and whites. Cynthia Nakashima observes that this is "a common theme, both in recent discussions of people of mixed race and in creative expression by people of mixed race."[78] The concept does not sit well with me. A bridge implies a connection between two levels of relatively equal ground. Although some argue that the bridge analogy reflects the need to translate cultures, such a translation often runs only one way. African Americans and other people of color already have some level of understanding of mainstream white culture; they *must* if they want to survive and thrive in the United States. In contrast, whites are not taught about the richness and beauty of black cultures or the cultures of other people of color. Moreover, in a society in which whites and blacks have unequal access to resources and power, in which whites are granted privileges and power based solely on skin color, multiracial family members need to act more like ladders than bridges. A ladder connects two communities yet takes into account racial inequity and holds members of multiracial families accountable to larger racial politics in society. As Angela Davis writes, "we must climb in such a way as to guarantee that all of our sisters, regardless of social class, and indeed all of our brothers, climb with us."[79]

# Conclusion

# *Challenging*

# *the Color*

# *Line*

Multiracial family members encounter two related obstacles when they attempt to address racial complexities and social justice simultaneously. The first obstacle involves their inability to articulate institutional forms of racism and the pervasiveness of white supremacy. We live in a society in which the social is reduced to the individual—that is, society does not have a race problem; individuals within society have one. Thus, many multiracial family members see border patrolling as an action between individuals: the border patroller and the victim. In such a construction, black and white border patrollers can each seem to be elements of a single-race "them" who victimizes the multiracial "us." Both seem equally racist when multiracials are the target. This leaves multiracials few alternatives other than to claim a new multiracial identity, community, and politic.[1] Charles Byrd speaks for many who find themselves in this position: "To those who say we're trying to create a new race, I submit that this 'new race' or 'new people,' if you will, was created centuries ago. . . . Lamentably, this 'new race' or 'new people' was initially swept under the rug by white racists. That practice is sadly carried out today by racists 'of color' in the name of numerical strength, and by their white political allies in the name of social segregation. In doing so, both deny us the right of self-determination and the right to name ourselves."²

In short, like Byrd, many multiracial family members choose not to recognize institutional forms of whiteness and racism and instead formulate a response to border patrolling, the form of discrimination they experience daily as individuals. But comparing black and white border patrolling implies that blacks have the social, economic, and political power necessary to determine the life chances of another group. While Byrd clearly is not ignoring race, his arguments share some basic themes with those who demand color-blind social policies. For instance, "both deny us the right of self-determination" implies that blacks and whites are on an equal footing in society. Further, the basis of his argument is that individuals be given this right of self-determination, which he privileges over group struggles for social justice. Similarly, color-blind advocates suggest that their policies protect individual liberties in a society in which race neither matters nor determines social outcomes.

Speaking on behalf of the Association of MultiEthnic Americans (AMEA), Carlos Fernandez testified before the Subcommittee on Census, Statistics, and Postal Personnel of the U.S. House of Representatives, arguing that the acceptance of a multiracial category would "avoid unnecessary and unwarranted government influence and interference in the very sensitive and private matter of personal identity."³ Like Byrd, Fernandez perceives individual liberties as more important than questions of social justice. I, however, agree with Dorothy Roberts, who suggests that "liberty protects all citizens' choices from the most direct and egregious abuses of government power, but it does nothing to dismantle social arrangements that make it impossible for some people to make a choice in the first place. Liberty guards against government intrusion; it does not guarantee social justice."[4] A movement that pushes the government toward a color blind platform while overwhelming racial injustice still exists is reproducing injustice. Instead of challenging essentialism and racism, the underlying constructs that lead to borderism, many multiracial family members demand government protection of their individual right to create the racial identities they desire.

The second obstacle is tied directly to the essentialist language through which most individuals frame race in the United States. After centuries of racial categorization, the color line seems clear. The language we have to talk about race makes racial boundaries and identities appear fixed, natural, and essential. Steeped in a western tradition of either-or thinking, our language leaves little room for addressing racial complexities and justice simultaneously. For instance, whites who claim a "no longer white" identity, family, and perhaps culture, still receive many of the privileges granted to whites. There is no positive language to describe a "no longer white" white. Those who step outside these categories appear to be unnatural and pathological.

Candace, the white mother of five grown multiracial children, worked in the public schools for years and has become very sensitive to the differing treatment she receives relative to her sons and her husband. She no longer identifies herself as white; but given the lack of language and the fact that she still receives privileges granted to whites, she is left without words to describe herself. She gave me an example. Several times she and her husband have been called to the police station about one or another of their sons who had been picked up for no apparent reason (other than appearance). She and her husband filed harassment charges against the police in several towns. Amid all this, on one rainy day she was driving home alone from the train station in a car that had only one headlight. She inadvertently drove out of an entrance-only road at the station. As she turned onto the street, she notice a police officer watching her from his car. The officer began to follow her. Certain she would be stopped for a double traffic violation, she began to reach for her license and registration. The officer followed her for about a mile until she turned into her driveway, but he did not stop her. "I was so mad. I knew my boys would have been stopped. I know my husband is stopped all the time. I know by rights I should be stopped and I'm not, and there's an anger that sets in." Each time Candace receives privileges while her husband and children face harassment, she is slapped with the reality that, no matter how she identifies herself, she is still considered white and still granted the privileges of whiteness. Each time this happens she is faced with the reality that a system of whiteness is in place, one that is detrimental to her family and to people of color in general. Essentialist language, racist institutions, and border patrollers protect a socially constructed system of white privilege by making the color line appear natural and immutable.

Candace, like many white partners in multiracial families, would prefer not to be seen as white, not to feel as though she was passing. Unfortunately, the language we have available perpetuates traditional racial categories while silencing those who attempt to move outside of them. Neil Gotanda asserts, "Under the American system of racial classification, claiming a white racial identity is a declaration of racial purity and an implicit assertion of racial domination."[5] Thus, while many whites may view interracially married whites as "no longer really white," the thinking stops there;

"not really white" is not a new category but an anti-category. These whites are not assigned new identities, nor is language available for them to describe new identities. Language available to describe multiracial family members is generally negative. As Maria P. P. Root reminds us, our limited border language limits our ability to talk about new identities.[6]

Essentialist thinking and language is so embedded in American society that even efforts to bring about greater social justice ultimately reproduce the color line that protects white privilege and power. For instance, recently I received a letter sealed with a sticker that read, "Teach tolerance." It was unsettling. What was I being asked to tolerate? Was I being asked to tolerate individual differences or social injustice? I began to think about how often this phrase is thrown around in diversity training seminars and among groups attempting to create better intergroup relations. In each case, tolerating individual differences is the goal. The motives behind the phrase may be all good, but to suggest that individual differences should be tolerated is problematic. Tolerance implies patience, "putting up with." Do we really want to suggest that we are just putting up with differences? What about respecting, appreciating, and learning about them? Tolerating is what we do in situations that feel intolerable. We tolerate levels of discomfort to finish marathons, give birth, finish degrees, raise a difficult child, and survive injustice. Those doing the tolerating, especially of other human beings, assume themselves to be superior, perhaps more powerful; they have the grace to tolerate what otherwise might be unbearable. Those being tolerated are belittled. I would rather not be around people who feel like they are tolerating me.

When larger racial (and other) inequalities are ignored, racial inequality is seen as merely racial difference. When "teach tolerance" is reduced to individual difference, this implies a leveling, a disregard for the ways in which differences are assigned value in the larger society. If "teach tolerance" is meant to address the larger historical and social context of race and difference in the United States, then this implies that people of color should tolerate the continued injustices of racism. After all, people with white skin and European features do not face racial injustice. They are privileged; they are not asked to put up with such injustices. After enduring centuries of inequality, are people of color now being asked to continue tolerating it?

At a minimum, however, "teach tolerance" challenges people to think about differences. The question then becomes how these differences are constructed. Are they viewed as biologically based or historically constructed and laced with power? I could suggest a competing slogan: "teach the social construction of racial categories." Certainly, it would not be an easy sell. It would take up an entire bumper. It's not easy to say and even more difficult to understand. But it might prompt an analysis of the social, historical, and political creation of race and injustice. It might challenge individuals to think about the ways in which power is central to race and racial categorization in the United States.

Like all social phenomena, race cannot be reduced to a single-factor analysis. Society is made up of the convergence of many factors and competing ideologies. The color line is being challenged, even as it is being reproduced, by those living on and across it as well as by those oppressed by it. At the same time, U.S. demographics are shifting. The broadly defined "people of color" group will shortly be the majority of Americans. Yet whites still maintain institutional power. Legislation, policies, and programs reflect the interests of those with the power to make and enforce decisions. A conservative Supreme Court is dismantling civil rights legislation case by case, and Congress is swiftly moving toward color-blind legislation.[7] Other considerations are the increasingly isolated poor black and Latino populations in large American cities. We have a punitive social welfare system while corporate welfare seems to flourish unabated. Taking a step back helps to bring into focus the control exercised by multinational corporations, some of which own the for-profit prisons into which the nation's poor are funneled.[8] The growth of free trade zones depends on the severely underpaid labor of large numbers of women, children, and some men who are making goods for consumers in the so-called first world. Most of the producers of these goods are women of color. When they flee the exploitative conditions in their countries of birth, they make their way to the United States to become the next group of exploited service workers, nannies, and sometimes sex workers. It is within this context that individuals must struggle to think about the complexities of social relations and justice. It is within this context that color lines are shifting.

Every semester I ask my freshman sociology students how many understand the difference between the Republican and Democratic parties. Out of a racially diverse class of thirty or so, one or two hands may go up. I ask them why they don't know. Secretly I am hoping they will suggest that Democrats have become more centrist, even conservative, making rhetoric and policy outcomes between the two parties very similar. Instead I hear, "We can't change anything anyway. Why bother?" "We were never taught this stuff." On hearing these responses, some individuals may be tempted to label these students as unmotivated and apathetic Gen X-ers. But I think these students do want to know, do want to feel powerful in a world in which power seems so ubiquitous and obfuscated at the same time. Like most people in the United States, they have been raised with binary thinking that impedes a more in-depth and critical understanding of race and social relations in society. The ambiguities of their lived experiences often contradict the tools they've been given to think about those experiences. As we talk about the lack of language and the shortcomings of western thought, the students begin to struggle to think in more critical and sophisticated ways. They begin to talk about their experiences and the social world as socially constructed. The categories, the borders, and the color line become a challenge for us all.

# Notes

## Introduction   *Thinking about the Color Line*

1. Mimi Abramowitz, *Regulating the Lives of Women: Social Welfare Policy from Colonial Times to the Present* (Boston: South End Press, 1996). See also Ian F. Haney Lopez, *White by Law: The Legal Construction of Race* (New York: New York University Press, 1996).
2. Naomi Zack, *Race and Mixed Race* (Philadelphia: Temple University Press, 1994), 22.
3. F. James Davis, *Who Is Black? One Nation's Definition* (University Park, Pa.: Penn State Press, 1991).
4. *Loving v. Virginia,* 388 U.S. 1 (1967).
5. Kim Ford-Mazrui, "Black Identity and Child Placement: The Best Interests of Black and Biracial Children" *Michigan Law Review* 92 (February 1994): 931.
6. Abby Ferber, "Exploring the Social Construction of Race," in *American Mixed Race: The Culture of Microdiversity*, ed. Naomi Zack (Lanham, Md.: Rowman and Littlefield, 1995), 160.
7. See, for instance, Susan Graham, "The Real World," in *The Multiracial Experience: Racial Borders As the New Frontier*, ed. Maria P. P. Root (Thousand Oaks, Calif.: Sage, 1996), 37–48.
8. Barbara Katz Rothman, *Genetic Maps and Human Imaginations: The Limits of Science in Understanding Who We Are* (New York: Norton, 1998), 116.
9. Kwame Anthony Appiah, "Racisms," in *Anatomy of Racism*, ed. David Theo Goldberg (St. Paul: University of Minnesota Press, 1990), 3–17.
10. Stuart Hall, "What Is This 'Black' in Black Popular Culture?" in *Black Popular Culture*, ed. Gina Dent (Seattle: Bay Press, 1992), 21–33.
11. Michael Omi and Howard Winant, *Racial Formation in the United States: From the 1960s to the 1990s*, 2d ed. (New York: Routledge and Kegan Paul, 1994).
12. Richard J. Hernstein and Charles Murray, *The Bell Curve: Intelli-*

*gence and Class Structure in American Life* (New York: Free Press, 1996).

13. Michael Eric Dyson, "Essentialism and the Complexities of Racial Identity," in *Multiculturalism: A Critical Reader*, ed. David Theo Goldberg (Cambridge, Mass.: Blackwell, 1994), 218–229. See also Appiah, "Racisms."

14. Lopez, *White by Law*, 14.

15. Abby Ferber, *White Man Falling: Race, Gender and White Supremacy* (Lanham, Md.: Rowman and Littlefield, 1998), 5.

16. Omi and Winant, *Racial Formation.*

17. Liberal humanists argue for color-blind policies because they believe race-based policies perpetuate racial significance and inequalities in society, thereby dividing the human community. Much of this writing has taken place within the context of trans-racial adoption debates. See, for instance, Randall Kennedy, "Orphans of Separatism: The Painful Politics of Transracial Adoption," *American Prospect* 17 (spring 1994): 38–45; Peter Hayes, "Transracial Adoption Politics and Ideology," *Child Welfare League of America* 72, 3 (1994): 301–310; and Elizabeth Bartholet, "Where Do Black Children Belong? The Politics of Race Matching in Adoption," *University of Pennsylvania Review* 139, 3 (1991): 1163–1256.

18. Yehudi O. Webster, *The Racialization of America* (New York: St. Martin's Press, 1993).

19. William Julius Wilson, *The Declining Significance of Race: Blacks and Changing American Institutions* (Chicago: University of Chicago Press, 1980).

20. Omi and Winant, *Racial Formation*, 31.

21. Quoted in Michael Novak, *Rise of the Unmeltable Ethnics* (New York: Macmillan, 1972), 47.

22. Ibid.; Heather Dalmage, "Factors of Integration: The Guatemalan Experience in Chicago," *Latino Studies* 4 (January 1993): 26.

23. See, for instance, Daniel Patrick Moynihan, "Employment, Income, and the Ordeal of the Negro Family," *Daedalus* 94 (fall 1965): 51. See also Hernstein and Murray, *The Bell Curve.*

24. Dyson, "Essentialism," 227.

25. Maureen Reddy, *Crossing the Color Line: Race, Parenting, and Culture* (New Brunswick, N. J.: Rutgers University Press, 1994), 32.

26. Ibid., 33.

27. bell hooks, *Black Looks: Race and Representation* (Boston: South End, 1992).

28. Golfer Tiger Woods invented the word *Cablinasian* to describe his various claimed heritages.

29. Maria P. P Root, "The Multiracial Experience: Racial Borders As a Significant Frontier in Race Relations," in *The Multiracial Experience*, xxiii.

30. Iris Marion Young, "The Ideal of Community and the Politics of Difference," in *Feminism/Postmodernism*, ed. Linda Nicholson

(New York: Routledge, 1990), 300–323; Sandra Harding, "Reinventing Ourselves As Other: More Agents of History and Knowledge," in *American Feminist Thought at Century's End: A Reader,* ed. Linda Kauffman (Cambridge, Mass.: Blackwell, 1993), 140–164; Liz Bondi, "Locating Identity Politics," in *Place and the Politics of Identity,* ed. Michael Keith and Steve Pile (New York: Routledge, 1993), 84–101.

31. Ruth Colker, *Hybrid: Bisexuals, Multiracials and Other Misfits under American Law* (New York: New York University Press, 1995).
32. See Root, *The Multiracial Experience.*
33. Kenya Mayfield, "Mixed-Race—The Next Generation," *Interrace* 6, 6 (1996): 22–25.
34. Root, *The Multiracial Experience.*
35. In an interview with Ray Suarez on National Public Radio's *Morning Edition* (15 November 1995), Lise Funderburg notes a similar finding in her research, speaking of public and private identities as a way to cope with demands for racial allegiance.
36. See, for instance, Maria P. P. Root's "Multiracial Bill of Rights," in *The Multiracial Experience,* 3–14.
37. Root, *The Multiracial Experience.*

## 1 *Discovering Racial Borders*

1. Gunnar Myrdal, *An American Dilemma: The Negro Problem and Modern Democracy,* 20th anniversary ed. (New York: Harper and Row, 1965 [1944]).
2. Abby Ferber, *White Man Falling: Race, Gender and White Supremacy* (Lanham, Md.. Rowman and Littlefield, 1998), 101.
3. Constance Perin, *Everything in Its Place: Social Order and Land Use in America* (Princeton, N. J.: Princeton University Press, 1977), 110–111.
4. Wayne West Gunthorpe, *Skin Color Recognition, Preference and Identification in Interracial Children: A Comparative Study* (Lanham, Md.: University Press of America, 1998); see also William E. Cross, *Shades of Black: Diversity in African-American Identity* (Philadelphia: Temple University Press, 1991).
5. Barbara Katz Rothman, *Genetic Maps and Human Imaginations: The Limits of Science in Understanding Who We Are* (New York: Norton, 1998), 51.
6. Grace Elizabeth Hale, *Making Whiteness: The Culture of Segregation in the South, 1890–1940* (New York: Vintage, 1998), 219.
7. See, for instance, Gloria Anzaldúa, *Borderlands/La Frontera: The New Mestiza* (San Francisco: Spinsters/Aunt Lute, 1987); Peter McLaren, "Border Disputes: Multicultural Narratives, Identity Formation, and Critical Pedagogy in Postmodern America," in *Naming Silenced Lives: Personal Narrative and the Process of*

*Educational Change,* ed. Daniel McLaughlin and William Tierney (New York: Routledge, 1993); and Maria P. P. Root, ed., *The Multiracial Experience: Racial Borders As the New Frontier* (Thousand Oaks, Calif.: Sage, 1996), xiii–xxviii.

8. Michael Omi and Howard Winant, *Racial Formation in the United States: From the 1960s to the 1990s,* 2d ed. (New York: Routledge and Kegan Paul, 1994).

9. For a detailed history, see Ian F. Haney Lopez, *White by Law: The Legal Construction of Race* (New York: New York University Press, 1996); and Omi and Winant, *Racial Formation.*

10. Hale, *Making Whiteness,* 238.

11. Omi and Winant, *Racial Formation;* Michael Eric Dyson, "Essentialism and the Complexities of Racial Identity," in *Multiculturalism: A Critical Reader,* ed. David Theo Goldberg (Cambridge, Mass.: Blackwell, 1994), 218–229; Lawrence Levine, *Black Culture and Black Consciousness: Afro-American Folk Thought from Slavery to Freedom* (New York: Oxford University Press, 1977).

12. Black women did not just make such choices; rather, they were coerced and given a limited set of opportunities. To imply otherwise is to romanticize the dehumanizing system they were forced into. See Paul Spikard, *Mixed Blood: Intermarriage and Ethnic Identity in Twentieth-Century America* (Madison: University of Wisconsin Press, 1989), 246.

13. Omi and Winant, *Racial Formation.*

14. Talk by Manning Marable, DePaul University, Chicago, 1991.

15. See Jonathon Kozol, *Savage Inequalities* (New York: Harper-Perennial, 1992).

16. bell hooks, *Black Looks: Race and Representation* (Boston: South End, 1992), 176.

17. See, for instance, Kozol, *Savage Inequalities.*

18. The outcome of these institutionalized practices can be seen in the emergence of the prison industrial complex. (Consider, for instance, Angela Davis's advocacy work.) Tied into this we have uneven drug laws and a race- and class-based death penalty enforcement that could be seen as modern versions of state-sanctioned racism, albeit dressed in a color-blind facade.

19. hooks, *Black Looks.*

20. Anzaldúa, *Borderlands/La Frontera.*

21. Hale, *Making Whiteness.*

22. Ruth Frankenberg, *White Women's Race Matters: The Social Construction of Whiteness* (Minneapolis: University of Minnesota, 1993).

23. Etienne Balibar and Immanuel Wallerstein, *Race, Nation, Class: Ambiguous Identities* (New York: Verso, 1991), 71.

24. Joe Feagin and Hernán Vera, *White Racism* (New York: Routledge, 1995), ix–x.

25. Ferber, *White Man Falling,* 100.

26. Naomi Zack, *Race and Mixed Race* (Philadelphia: Temple University Press, 1994).

27. Mimi Abramowitz, *Regulating the Lives of Women: Social Welfare Policy from Colonial Times to the Present* (Boston: South End Press, 1996).

28. Ibid., 3.

29. Valerie Babb, *Whiteness Visible: The Meaning of Whiteness in American Literature and Culture* (New York: New York University Press, 1998), 76.

30. Hale, *Making Whiteness*, 109.

31. See, for instance, Gail Folaron and McCartt Hess, "Placement Considerations for Children of Mixed African American and Caucasian Parentage," *Child Welfare League of America* 72, 3 (1993): 113–135.

32. See, for instance, Ferber, *White Man Falling*.

33. Ibid.

34. Ibid., 104.

35. Robert Merton, "Intermarriage and the Social Structure: Fact and Theory," *Psychiatry* 4 (1941): 361–374; see also Matthijs Kalmijn, "Trends in Black/White Intermarriage," *Social Forces* 72, 1 (1996): 119–146.

36. Merton, "Intermarriage"; Kingsley Davis, "Intermarriage in Caste Societies," *American Anthropologist* (September 1941): 388–395.

37. Ferber, *White Man Falling*.

38. Zack, *Race and Mixed Race*; Joel Williamson, *New People: Miscegenation and Mulattoes in the United States* (New York: New York University Press, 1984); Spikard, *Mixed Blood*.

39. Ferber, *White Man Falling*, 103.

40. Kate Davy, "Outing Whiteness." *Theatre* 47, 2 (1995): 189–205.

41. Charles Gallagher, "White Reconstruction in the University," *Socialist Review* 24, 1 and 2 (1995): 165–188.

42. Cathy J. Cohen, "Contested Membership: Black Gay Identities and the Politics of AIDS," in *Queer Theory/Sociology*, ed. Steven Seidman (Cambridge, Mass.: Blackwell, 1996), 365.

43. Frantz Fanon, *Black Skins, White Masks* (New York: Grove), 83.

44. Ibid., 60.

45. Paul C. Rosenblatt, Terri A. Karis, and Richard D. Powell, *Multiracial Couples: Black and White Voices* (Thousand Oaks, Calif.: Sage, 1995), 155.

46. Dyson, "Essentialism," 222.

47. Rosenblatt et al., *Multiracial Couples*, 150.

48. Ibid., 151.

49. Ibid.

50. Gloria Wade-Gayles, *Rooted against the Wind* (Boston: Beacon, 1996), 110.

51. David Heer, "Negro-White Marriages in the United States," *Journal of Marriage and the Family* 28 (1966): 262–273; Kalmijn,

"Trends"; Merton, "Intermarriage"; Davis, "Intermarriage in Caste Societies."
52. Frankenberg, *White Women*, 112.
53. James McBride, *The Color of Water: A Black Man's Tribute to His White Mother* (New York: Riverhead, 1996), 16.
54. Maria P. P. Root, "The Multiracial Contribution to the Browning of America," in *American Mixed Race: The Culture of Microdiversity*, ed. Naomi Zack (Lanham, Md.: Rowman and Littlefield, 1995), 234.
55. Jane Lazarre thinks of herself as a person of color, and Maureen Reddy writes of "masquerading as white in public." See Lazarre, *Beyond the Whiteness of Whiteness: Memoir of a White Mother of Black Sons* (Durham, N. C.: Duke University Press, 1996); and Reddy, *Crossing the Color Line: Race, Parenting, and Culture* (New Brunswick, N.J.: Rutgers University Press, 1994), 22.
56. hooks, *Black Looks*, 177.
57. Although many people break up permanently, I interviewed individuals who eventually made the decision to commit to an interracial marriage.
58. Claudette Bennett, "Interracial Children: Implications for a Multiracial Category" (paper presented at the annual meeting of the American Sociological Association, Washington, D.C., 1995).
59. Rosenblatt et al., *Multiracial Couples*, 5.

## 2   Redlines and Color Lines

1. Douglas Massey and Nancy Denton, *American Apartheid: Segregation and the Making of the Underclass* (Cambridge: Harvard University Press, 1993).
2. Philip Nyden, John Lukehart, Michael Maly, and William Peterman, "Neighborhood Racial and Ethnic Diversity in U.S. Cities," *Cityscape* 4, 2 (1998): 1–17.
3. Paul Hancock, "Mortgage Lending Discrimination" (paper presented at the John Marshall Law School Fair Housing Center's Mortgage Lending Discrimination and Insurance Redlining Conference, Chicago, 19 April 1996).
4. John E. Taylor, "Importance of Community Reinvestment Act to Traditionally Underserved Communities" (paper presented at the John Marshall Law School Fair Housing Center's Mortgage Lending Discrimination and Insurance Redlining Conference, Chicago, 19 April 1996).
5. Manning Marable, "Beyond Color-Blindness," *The Nation*, 28 December 1998, 12.
6. Gregory Squires, *Capital and Communities in Black and White: The Intersection of Race, Class and Uneven Development* (Albany: State University of New York Press, 1994).
7. Massey and Denton, *American Apartheid*.

8. Karl E. Taeuber and Alma F. Taeuber, *Negroes in Cities: Residential Segregation and Neighborhood Change.* (Chicago: Aldine, 1965).

9. Massey and Denton, *American Apartheid.*

10. Peter Wood and Barrett Lee, "Is Neighborhood Racial Succession Inevitable? Forty Years of Evidence," *Urban Affairs Quarterly* 26, 4 (1991): 610–620.

11. Massey and Denton, *American Apartheid;* Carol Goodwin, *The Oak Park Strategy* (Chicago: University of Chicago Press, 1979).

12. Gregory Squires, Larry Bennett, Kathleen McCourt, and Philip Nyden, *Chicago: Race, Class, and the Response to Urban Decline* (Philadelphia: Temple University Press, 1987), 54.

13. Ibid., 53.

14. Constance Perin details the continuing connection that realtors and developers make between homogeneity, property values, and social conflict: "People who 'live among their own' . . . are making use of strategies that can, sensibly, lessen the effort and time it takes to work out many intrinsic conflicts of social life." She suggest that diversity leads to greater probability of conflict. The unwritten text is that homogeneity in the housing market works to the advantage of whites and the disadvantage of blacks and leaves multiracial families with few options. See Perin, *Everything in Its Place: Social Order and Land Use in America* (Princeton, N. J.: Princeton University Press, 1977), 85.

15. Arnold Hirsch, *Making the Second Ghetto: Race and Housing in Chicago, 1940–1960* (New York: Cambridge University Press), 1983.

16. With their life savings tied to the value of their property, working-class whites fear losing that value. Without stocks, bonds, and other forms of wealth to draw on in times of need, they see a house as their safety net. It is easy for panic peddlers to use racist ideologies to scare working-class whites into selling.

17. For a wonderful analysis of the connection between nationalist movements and the continued struggle for social justice, see Waneema Lubiano, "Black Nationalism and Black Common Sense" in *The House That Race Built*, ed. Waneema Lubiano, 232–252 (New York: Vintage, 1997).

18. Pierre Bourdieu, *Distinction: A Social Critique of the Judgement of Taste* (Cambridge: Harvard University Press, 1984).

19. Cynthia Nakashima, "The Invisible Monster: The Creation and Denial of Mixed-Race People in America," in *Racially Mixed People in America*, ed. Maria P. P. Root, (Newbury Park, Calif.: Sage, 1992),162–178.

20. Ibid., 174.

21. Lisa Jones, *Bulletproof Diva: Tales of Race, Sex and Hair* (New York: Doubleday, 1994), 60.

22. Angela Davis, "Discussion," in *What's Black in Black Popular Culture*, ed. Gina Dent (Seattle: Bay, 1992), 328.

23. Jones, *Bulletproof Diva*, 60.
24. Perin, *Everything*; Squires et al., *Chicago*.
25. Squires, *Capital and Communities*, 59.
26. Kenneth T. Jackson, *Crabgrass Frontiers: The Suburbanization of the United States* (New York: Oxford University Press, 1985).
27. Squires et al., *Chicago*, 101.
28. Perin, *Everything*.
29. *Fair Housing Act*, 100th Congress, 2d session, H.R. 1158.
30. Squires et al., *Chicago*; Jackson, *Crabgrass Frontiers*, 71.
31. Lillian Seymour, "Fair Housing Audits" (paper presented at the John Marshall Law School Fair Housing Center's Mortgage Lending Discrimination and Insurance Redlining Conference, Chicago, 19 April 1996).
32. Paul C. Rosenblatt, Terri A. Karis, and Richard D. Powell, *Multiracial Couples: Black and White Voices* (Thousand Oaks, Calif.: Sage, 1995).
33. The fact that all the children stopped speaking with Mark may not have been racially motivated, although he was unable to explain it in any other way. His suspicion that it was race-based was confirmed when he moved to Montclair and made many friends.
34. Gunnar Myrdal, *An American Dilemma: The Negro Problem and Modern Democracy*, 20th anniversary ed. (New York: Harper and Row, 1965 [1944]); Juliet Saltman, "Neighborhood Stabilization: A Fragile Movement," *Sociological Quarterly* 31, 4 (1990): 531–549.
35. Hirsch, *Making the Second Ghetto*; Wood and Lee, "Is Neighborhood Racial Succession Inevitable?"
36. Squires et al., *Chicago*.
37. Andrew Hacker, *Two Nations: Black and White, Separate, Hostile, Unequal* (New York: Scribner's, 1992); Massey and Denton, *American Apartheid*.
38. Franklin Frazier, "The Negro Middle Class and Desegregation," *Social Problems* 4 (April 1957): 165–178; Marable, "Beyond Color-Blindness."
39. Juliet Saltman, "Maintaining Racially Diverse Neighborhoods," *Urban Affairs Quarterly* 26, 3 (1991): 416–441.
40. Nyden et al., "Diversity in U.S. Cities."
41. Ibid., 10.
42. Ibid., 11.
43. Ibid.
44. See, for instance, bell hooks, *Black Looks: Race and Representation* (Boston: South End, 1992), 21–39.
45. Stan West, "Is Oak Park Really Integrated?" *Journal Express*, 21 February 1996, 27.
46. Lise Funderburg, *Black, White, Other: Biracial Americans Talk about Race* (New York: Morrow, 1994).
47. See the proceedings of the John Marshall Law School Fair Housing

Center's Mortgage Lending Discrimination and Insurance Redlining Conference, Chicago, 19 April 1996.

## 3  The Nation's Racial Rorschach Tests

1. Peter Caws, "Identity: Cultural, Transcultural and Multicultural," in *Multiculturalism: A Critical Reader*, ed. David Theo Goldberg (Cambridge, Mass.: Blackwell, 1994), 378.
2. Prenatal treatment and the treatment the parents receive during pregnancy are determined by social categories. It may be more appropriate to say "from conception." However such a statement is loaded with meanings and may be a topic for another book.
3. Michael Omi and Howard Winant, *Racial Formation in the United States: From the 1960s to the 1990s*, 2d ed. (New York: Routledge and Kegan Paul, 1994), 60.
4. Teresa Kay Williams, "Race As Process: Reassessing the 'What Are You?' Encounters of Biracial Individuals," in *The Multiracial Experience: Racial Borders As the New Frontier*, ed. Maria P. P. Root (Thousand Oaks, Calif.: Sage, 1996), 203.
5. Lise Funderburg, *Black, White, Other: Biracial Americans Talk about Race* (New York: Morrow, 1994); Maria P. P. Root, ed., *Racially Mixed People in America* (Newbury Park, Calif.: Sage, 1992), 342–347; Julie Lythcott-Haims, "Where Do Mixed Babies Belong? Racial Classification in America and Its Implications for Transracial Adoption," *Harvard Civil Rights–Civil Liberties Law Review* 29, 4 (1994): 531–558.
6. Williams, "Race As Process," 208.
7. Omi and Winant, *Racial Formation*.
8. Carla Bradshaw, "Beauty and the Beast: On Racial Ambiguity," in Root, *Racially Mixed People*, 88.
9. Naomi Zack, *Race and Mixed Race* (Philadelphia: Temple University Press, 1994).
10. Cecilia Goodnow, "Greeting Cards Target Interracial Families," *Chicago Tribune*, 20 June 1995, 16.
11. Candy Mills, "Editor's Note," *Interrace Magazine* 6, 6 (1996): 2.
12. Kathy Russell, Midge Wilson, and Ronald Hall, *The Color Complex: The Politics of Skin Color among African Americans* (New York: Harcourt Brace Jovanovich, 1992), 31.
13. Ibid., 34.
14. Manning Marable, "Race, Identity, and Political Culture," in *Black Popular Culture*, ed. Gina Dent (Seattle: Bay, 1992), 295–296.
15. Danzy Senna "Mulatto Millennium," in *Half + Half: Writers Growing Up Biracial and Bicultural*, ed. Claudine Chiawei O'Hearn (New York: Pantheon, 1998), 16.
16. Kathy Odell Korgen, *From Black to Biracial: Transforming Racial Identity among Americans* (Westport, Conn.: Praeger, 1998), 43.

17. Marable, "Race, Identity, and Political Culture," 301.
18. Ibid., 295.
19. Abby Ferber, *White Man Falling: Race, Gender and White Supremacy* (Lanham, Md.: Rowman and Littlefield, 1998).
20. Neil Gotanda, "A Critique of 'Our Constitution Is Color-Blind,' " in *Critical Race Theory*, ed. Kimberlé Crenshaw, Neil Gotanda, Gary Peller, and Kendall Thomas (New York: New Press, 1995), 259.
21. Lisa Jones, *Bulletproof Diva: Tales of Race, Sex and Hair* (New York: Doubleday, 1994), 34.
22. Senna, "Mulatto Millennium," 18.
23. Ibid.
24. Walter White, *A Man Called White* (New York: Viking, 1948), 3.
25. Ibid., 51.
26. Judith Scales Trent, *Notes of a White Black Woman: Race, Color, Community* (University Park, Pa.: Penn State University Press, 1995), 3.

## 4  Communities, Politics, and Racial Thinking

1. See Benedict Anderson, *Imagined Communities: Reflections on the Origin and Spread of Nationalism* (New York: Verso, 1991).
2. See the case of Susie Phipps in Michael Omi and Howard Winant, *Racial Formation in the United States: From the 1960s to the 1990s*, 2d ed. (New York: Routledge and Kegan Paul, 1994), 53–54.
3. Neil Gotanda, "A Critique of 'Our Constitution is Color-Blind,' " in *Critical Race Theory*, ed. Kimberlé Crenshaw, Neil Gotanda, Gary Peller, and Kendall Thomas (New York: New Press, 1995), 260.
4. See, for instance, Lavonne Gaddy's written testimony to the Committee on Government Reform and Oversight of the U.S. House of Representatives, 29 January 1999.
5. Cynthia Nakashima, "Voices from the Movement: Approaches to Multiraciality," in *The Multiracial Experience: Racial Borders As the New Frontier*, ed. Maria P. P. Root, (Thousand Oaks, Calif.: Sage, 1996), 79–97.
6. Ibid., 82.
7. Barbara Katz Rothman, "Transracial Adoption: Refocusing Upstream" (paper presented at Color Lines in the Twenty-First Century, Chicago, 28 September 1998).
8. Charles Byrd, speech delivered at the multiracial solidarity march, Washington, D.C., 20 July 1996.
9. As of January 2000, the BFN will change its name to one that both honors its founder, Irene Carr, and reflects the multiracial experience.
10. These comments are based on an interview with one of the cofounders of the original GIFT in Central New Jersey.
11. Ibid.

12. "Mark Your Calendar," *GIFT Newsletter* (March 1996): 2.
13. Individual members of the organization can be politically involved but not on behalf of the organization.
14. See, for instance, Lisa Jones, *Bulletproof Diva: Tales of Race, Sex and Hair* (New York: Doubleday, 1994); Karen Grisby Bates, "The Trouble with the Rainbow: Will Blackness Have a Place in a Truly Multiracial America?" *Utne Reader* 6 (November/December 1994):12–14; Harold L. Hodgkinson, "What Should We Call People? Race, Class, and the Census for 2000," *Phi Delta Kappan* (October 1995): 173–179; and Lawrence Wright, "One Drop of Blood," *New Yorker*, 25 July 1994, 46–49.
15. Luis Rodriguez, *Always Running, La Vida Loca: Gang Days in L.A.* (New York: Touchstone, 1993), 8.
16. Nancy Brown and Ramona Douglass, "Making the Invisible Visible: The Growth of Community Network Organizations," in Root, ed., *The Multiracial Experience*, 323–340.
17. Ibid.
18. Ibid., 330.
19. Ramona Douglass, "AMEA's Appointment to the 2000 Census Advisory Committee," *Interracial/Intercultural Connection* 14, 2 (1996): 2.
20. Two other multiracial family organizations exist in the suburbs of Chicago: the Biracial Family Network of Oak Park and the Interracial Family Network of Evanston.
21. Suzann Evinger, "How Shall We Measure Our Nation's Diversity," *Chance* 8, 1 (1995): 7–14.
22. See Sally Katzen, "Notice," *Federal Register, Part IV, Office of Management and Budget, Standards for Classification of Federal Data on Race and Ethnicity* 59, 110 (1994): 14872.
23. Maria Puente, "Census 2000: Countdown to the Millennium," *USA Today*, 2 January 1996, 10.
24. Julie Lythcott-Haims, "Where Do Mixed Babies Belong? Racial Classification in America and Its Implications for Transracial Adoption," *Harvard Civil Rights–Civil Liberties Law Review* 29 (1994): 531–558; Ruth Colker, *Hybrid: Bisexuals, Multiracials and Other Misfits under American Law* (New York: New York University Press, 1995).
25. Douglass, "AMEA's Appointment."
26. Byrd, speech. The goal was to bring together multiracial people, present a united front, and demand recognition from the government and the nation.
27. Jane Ayers Chiong, *Racial Categorization of Multiracial Children in Schools* (Westport, Conn.: Bergin and Harvey, 1998), 111.
28. Ramona Douglass, "Freedom to Choose," an open letter from the AMEA president, posted at http://www.ameasite.org, 30 October 1997.

29. See, for instance, Christine Iijima Hall, "Coloring Outside the Lines," in *Racially Mixed People in America,* ed. Maria P. P. Root, 326–329 (Newbury Park, Calif.: Sage, 1992); and Byrd, speech.
30. See, for instance, Susan Graham, "Grassroots Advocacy," in *American Mixed Race: The Culture of Microdiversity,* ed. Naomi Zack (Lanham, Md.: Rowman and Littlefield, 1995), 185–189.
31. Lise Funderburg, *Black, White, Other: Biracial Americans Talk about Race* (New York: Morrow, 1994); Stuart Hall, "Ethnicity: Identity and Difference" (speech delivered at Hampshire College, Amherst, Massachusetts, spring 1989); Peter Caws, "Identity: Cultural, Transcultural and Multicultural," in *Multiculturalism: A Critical Reader,* ed. David Theo Goldberg (Cambridge, Mass.: Blackwell, 1994).
32. Byrd, speech.
33. Project RACE, "Urgent Medical Concerns," posted at http://projectrace.home.mindspring.com, 1997.
34. Ramona Douglass, speech delivered at the Multiracial Solidarity March, Washington, D.C., 20 July 1996.
35. Project RACE, "Urgent Medical Concerns," posted at http://projectrace.home.mindspring.com, 1997.
36. Hodgkinson, "What Should We Call People?" 170–173. Hodgkinson, director of the Center for Demographic Policy at the Institute for Educational Leadership, projects that if the multiracial category had been approved for Census 2000 and was to include anyone of "any racial/ethnic mixing four or more generations," then up to 80 percent of blacks and a majority of Americans would be considered and consider themselves multiracial.
37. In fact, it was believed that mulattos (translated as "mules") were a new and different breed unable to reproduce offspring.
38. Kathy Odell Korgen, *From Black to Biracial: Transforming Identity among Americans* (Westport, Conn.: Praeger, 1998), 105.
39. Byrd, speech.
40. Lythcott-Haims, "Where Do Mixed Race Babies Belong?" 540–541.
41. Jones, *Bulletproof Diva,* 57.
42. Bates, "The Trouble with the Rainbow."
43. Lise Funderburg, interview with Ray Suarez on National Public Radio's *Morning Edition,* 15 November 1995.
44. Ibid.
45. Jon Michael Spencer, *The New Colored People: The Mixed-Race Movement in America* (New York: New York University Press, 1997), 159.
46. Ibid.
47. Byrd, speech.
48. Gary Peller, "Race-Consciousness," in *Critical Race Theory,* ed. Kimberlé Crenshaw, Neil Gotanda, Gary Peller, and Kendall Thomas (New York: New Press, 1995), 149.
49. Byrd, speech.

50. Jones, *Bulletproof Diva*, 58.
51. Maria P. P. Root, "The Multiracial Contribution to the Browning of America," in Zack, ed., *American Mixed Race*, 231–236.
52. G. Reginald Daniel, "Beyond Black and White: The New Multiracial Consciousness," in Root, ed., *Racially Mixed People in America*, 333–341.
53. Dorothy Roberts, *Killing the Black Body: Race, Reproduction, and the Meaning of Liberty* (New York: Pantheon, 1997).
54. Ibid., 276; see also Rita Simon, Howard Altstein, and Marygold Meli, *The Case for Transracial Adoption* (Washington, D. C.: American University Press, 1994).
55. Leon Chestang, "The Dilemma of Biracial Adoption," *Social Work* 17 (May 1972): 100–105.
56. Peter Hayes, "Transracial Adoption Politics and Ideology," *Child Welfare League of America* 72, 3 (1994): 304, 308.
57. Roberts, *Killing the Black Body*.
58. Yehudi O. Webster, *The Racialization of America* (New York: St. Martin's Press, 1993); Randall Kennedy, "Orphans of Separatism: The Painful Politics of Transracial Adoption," *American Prospect* 17 (spring 1994): 38–45; Elizabeth Bartholet, "Where Do Black Children Belong? The Politics of Race Matching in Adoption," *University of Pennsylvania Review* 139, 3 (1991): 1163–1256; Hayes, "Transracial Adoptions."
59. Kennedy, "Orphans of Separatism," 40.
60. Simon et al., *The Case for Transracial Adoption*.
61. Webster, *Racialization of America*, 73.
62. Gotanda, "A Critique," 257.
63. Simon et al., *The Case for Transracial Adoption*, 39.
64. Ibid., 15.
65. Omi and Winant, *Racial Formation*.
66. National Association of Black Social Workers, *Position Statement* (February 1986), 31.
67. National Association of Black Social Workers, *Position Statement* (April 1994), 1.
68. Iris Marion Young, "The Ideal of Community and the Politics of Difference," in *Feminism/Postmodernism*, ed. Linda Nicholson (New York: Routledge, 1990) , 300–323.
69. See, for instance, Simon et al., *The Case for Transracial Adoption*.
70. Several individuals in interracial marriages spoke of "concerned family and friends" who made comments such as "You two may be strong enough to handle this, but is it fair to put this on a child?" or "I think it's okay for people to date interracially, but they shouldn't get married. That's irresponsible given what the children will be forced to endure."
71. Bartholet, "Where Do Black Children Belong?"
72. Ibid., 1187, note 60.
73. I did not interview anyone with two socially defined African

American birth parents who was then adopted by a white family. The transracially adopted adults with whom I spoke were all between the ages of twenty-four and forty-two. Each had one white and one black birth parent. My sample reflects a pattern in transracial adoptions. Bartholet explains that transracial adoptions tend to "involve children who are in fact biracial or multiracial and relatively light rather than dark skinned. . . .The theory has been that these kinds of placements constitute less of a breach with same-race matching principles than would placement of the 'pure' black child with white parents" (ibid., 1175–1176, note 14).

74. Gail Folaron and Peg McCartt Hess, "Placement Considerations for Children of Mixed African American and Caucasian Parentage," *Child Welfare League of America* 72, 3 (1993):120.
75. Ibid., 118.
76. Ibid., 119.
77. Simon et al., *The Case for Transracial Adoption.*
78. Nakashima, "Voices from the Movement," 89.
79. Angela Davis, *Women, Culture, and Politics* (New York: Vintage, 1990), 5.

## Conclusion    Challenging the Color Line

1. Byrd, speech delivered at the multiracial solidarity march, Washington, D. C., 20 July 1996.
2. Ibid.
3. Carlos Fernandez, "Testimony of the Association of MultiEthnic Americans before the Subcommittee on Census, Statistics, and Postal Personnel of the U.S. House of Representatives," in *American Mixed Race: The Culture of Microdiversity*, ed. Naomi Zack (Lanham, Md.: Rowman and Littlefield, 1995), 195.
4. Dorothy Roberts, *Killing the Black Body: Race, Reproduction, and the Meaning of Liberty* (New York: Pantheon, 1997), 294.
5. Neil Gotanda, "A Critique of 'Our Constitution Is Color-Blind,' " in *Critical Race Theory*, ed. Kimberlé Crenshaw, Neil Gotanda, Gary Peller, and Kendall Thomas (New York: New Press, 1995), 259.
6. Maria P. P. Root, ed., *The Multiracial Experience: Racial Borders As the New Frontier* (Thousand Oaks, Calif.: Sage, 1996), xxiii.
7. See, for instance, David Cole, *No Equal Justice: Race and Class in the American Criminal Justice System* (New York: New Press, 1999).
8. See Robin D. G. Kelley, *Yo' Mama's Disfunktional! Fighting the Cultural Wars in Urban America* (Boston: Beacon, 1997).

# Index

Massey, Douglas, 71, 74
*Michigan Law Review*, 6
*Mixed Blood* (Spikard), 36–37
mixed racial identity, 24–25
movies, multiracial actors in,
    110–111
"Mulatto Milennium" (Senna),
    112, 120
multiethnic identity label,
    25–26
multiracial categories. *See*
    census categories
multiracial community:
    defining, 131; formal
    organizations, 136–143;
    informal networks,
    134–136; as response to
    border patrolling, 132,
    171–172; *vs* single-race
    socializing, 133–134; social
    justice component for,
    132–133
*Multiracial Experience, The*
    (Root), 145
multiracial identity label, 1–2, 6
multiracial resources, lack of,
    109–110
Myrdal, Gunnar, 33, 95

Nakashima, Cynthia, 80, 132,
    170
National Association of Black
    Social Workers (NABSW),
    154, 155, 159
National Association of
    Realtors, 75
National Committee on Vital
    and Health Statistics, 147

National Neighbors, 96
*New Colored People, The: The
    Mixed-Race Movement in
    America* (Spencer), 152
New York City, housing
    segregation in, 73–74
Njeri, Itabari, 152
nuclear family, 4

Office of Management and
    Budget (OMB), and census
    racial categories, 143–144,
    145, 147
Omi, Michael, 13–14, 106
one-drop rule, 5, 6, 149–150
organizations, multiracial,
    136–143

patriarchy, 45, 48
Peller, Gary, 153
Perin, Constance, 34–35, 88
police harassment, 19, 65–66
Project RACE, 147

race: as border, 34–40 (*see also*
    borderism); color-blind
    view of, 13–15; critical
    understanding of, 176–178;
    demographics of, 176;
    essentialist view of (*see*
    essentialist thinking);
    loyalty, 57, 60; and power,
    51, 52, 58–59; recognition,
    35, 117; social construc-
    tionist view of, 11–13;
    white avoidance of, 38–40,
    50, 117–118. *See also* racial
    identity; racism

# About the Author

Heather M. Dalmage is the director of the Mansfield Institute for Social Justice and an associate professor of sociology at Roosevelt University. She has won the David Spitz Distinguished Scholar Fellowship for her study of multiracial families. She lives in Chicago with her husband and daughter.